PASS NOTES

PASS NOTES

theguardian

FOREWORD

by

TIM DOWLING

Published by
Galileo Publishers
16 Woodlands Road,
Great Shelford,
Cambridge CB22 5LW

www.galileopublishing.co.uk
Galileo Publishers is an imprint of Galileo Multimedia Ltd.

ISBN   978-1-903385-48-7

First edition

Printed in Lithuania
Cover by NM Design

CONTENTS

Foreword by Tim Dowling

Even after all the years I've been contributing to Pass Notes, one basic step in its manufacture remains a mystery to me: I've never understood the process by which the day's subject is chosen. I just get an email in the morning telling me what it is, followed by a wholly rhetorical "Does that sound OK?" The selected topic might be a well known public figure, or a commonly understood concept: summer, baby talk, Wales. But more often than not it's a word or phrase that means nothing to me.

One thing is always certain: I will end the day knowing a lot more about Jar Jar Binks – or Jammie Dodgers, or Transcranial Direct Current Stimulation, or coffee pods or the Marquess of Bath – than I ever thought I wanted to know. Pass Notes may be a handy distillation of the relevant facts, but I invariably end up with a great number of irrelevant facts stuck in my head. If a dinner party conversation turns to the subject of coffee pods, you don't want to be sitting next to me.

If the distillation is the hard part of the job, it's also the most important. From the beginning Pass Notes had a mission to inform as well as entertain, to present everything you need to know about a given subject in fewer than 400 words. It is this obligation to educate that, perversely, makes some people wonder whether the column is a sophisticated satire of our dumbed-down factoid culture, or just another symptom of it. I can't speak for everyone who has ever written a Pass Notes, but personally, I'm determined to have it both ways.

When I first encountered Pass Notes – this would have been in 1992 – I was an instant fan. It was that rare thing: an example of newspaper humour that was actually funny. The idea itself originated in the short-lived *Sunday Correspondent*, which closed its doors in 1990. After a suitable period of mourning, Pass Notes was resurrected for a page 3 slot in the *Guardian's* brand new G2 section. It was produced, then as now, by a rota of anonymous *Guardian* writers.

If I was impressed, I was also envious. I thought to myself: "I could do that." At the time I was a young and unsuccessful freelance journalist, and writing Pass Notes became an unspoken ambition. It would be almost ten years before I got the chance. Perhaps I should have spoken up sooner.

In the beginning – 3,700-something Pass Notes ago – the format was a little different. While it was very much the crib sheet for the modern age that it remains, it tended to be presented from a single authorial perspective. It took a while for the column to develop its unique – and when you think about it, deeply weird – conceit: the Q and the A gradually became two distinct voices. They developed personality traits – insolence, impatience, self-righteousness - that could vary or shift depending on the requirements of the subject, but even in the early days this nameless, faceless pair came to share a disregard for the strictures of the Pass Notes formula. Part of the fun of writing it is the struggle to keep them in line.

Because Pass Notes is penned anonymously (apart from a very brief period when it returned to G2 after a 4-year hiatus), it's a safe place to parade your own prejudices and stupidities. To do justice to both voices you must summon up your inner pedant as well as your inner moron. In the guise of the ignorant one who asks all the questions, I can admit that I still get my Dimblebys and Attenboroughs mixed up. I can confess that I don't know what Katy Perry's been up to lately, or indeed ever. And if you can't mansplain in a Pass Notes, when can you?

It is always tempting to let the two voices run away with the show, but it's never a good idea. Many great comic writers have contributed to Pass Notes over the past quarter century – Matthew Norman, Catherine Bennett and Lucy Mangan among them – and the best know that the questioner and the answerer must be made to play by the rules. If they occasionally go off-message, they have to stay on-topic. As the venerable and prolific Pass Notes contributor Stephen Moss once wrote: "If it becomes a slanging match, then the column has probably failed. They are not the stars; the subject is."

The format, too, may be occasionally bent, but never broken. The rigid structure of Pass Notes is the key to its success. In many ways it's an exercise in comedic form-filling. It's to the formula's enduring credit that most of the time I can't tell which of my colleagues has written that day's instalment. Sometimes I can't remember which ones I've written. Should an author ever play too fast and loose with the column's established conventions, the *Guardian's* feature editors are tireless defenders of tradition. Try putting the "Don't say" before the "Do say" for no good reason, and you will feel their wrath.

That's not to say there isn't room for playful innovation within the confines of the format. I wish I could say it was me who, obliged to put down something under "age" in a Pass Notes on mud, wrote "fractionally younger than soil and water." Whomever it was, I salute them.

It's not easy, but you can always find a different way to do the same thing. That's why, after all these years, I never get tired of writing Pass Notes, and I never get tired of reading it.

Tim Dowling, September 2016

~ GATWICK AIRPORT ~

Age: 51.

Appearance: January sales, with planes.

Ah, Gatwick, gateway to Aalborg, Aberdeen, Accra and 200 places that don't begin with A! Does any name so conjure up the glamour of travel? "Blofeld's stolen two nuclear warheads and we need you in Nassau, 007. There's a car waiting to take you to Gatwick."

Very droll. What's the place really like? Have you ever been to Oxford Street on a Saturday afternoon? More than 30 million passengers pass through Gatwick every year, and Harrods, Hamleys, Hugo Boss and dozens of other retailers are waiting to strip them of their worthless British pounds. "There's so much more to air travel than just flying," the airport's website declares. That tedious getting-on to-planes business is less well catered for. "For years," Virgin Atlantic complained yesterday, "the airport has suffered from a lack of investment." The last major work, in 2005, created 11 new "pier-served stands", whatever they are, and a bridge so big you can drive a 747 under it.

Planes are bigger now, aren't they? Can Gatwick afford a higher bridge? Global Infrastructure Partners (GIP), which owns the bijou and startingly well-run London City Airport, is buying Gatwick for £1.5bn and says it will "upgrade and modernise" it.

Is £1.5bn a good price? Gatwick – the name means 'goat farm' – dates back to the 13th century. Planes have been landing here since the 1930s, when it was the home of the Surrey Aero Club. The present facility was opened by the Queen in 1958. How can you put a price on history?

Have a go. Well, the owner, BAA, was hoping for more, but a) it has almost £10bn of debt and can't be too picky and b) the Competition Commission has ordered it to get rid of three airports. Poor old GIP, meanwhile, thought it was paying 99p and didn't check the small print about taxes and handling charges.

Do say: "This really is a unique retail experience."

Don't say: "I didn't get a cavity search the last time I went to Tie Rack."

22/10/2009

~ ANTIBIOTIC-FREE MEAT ~

Age: Brand new.

Appearance: A smiling pig's face.

Oh good, I'm so hungry. Are you? Hungry for meat?

Yes, I love meat! Yum! Meat that has been intensively farmed? If so, there is a very strong chance that it has been systematically pumped full of antibiotics.

Good! I don't want to eat a poorly animal. It's not so much because they're poorly, more that the antibiotics – when administered in subtherapeutic doses – improve feed conversion efficiency. They might be brimming with penicillin or bambermycin or salinomycin or virginiamycin or carbadox, all because they make the animal bigger.

Thank God for that! Big animals means more meat for me! That's not a good thing. All these antibiotics are entering the food chain. They are in your body now.

Great! I'll never be ill again! You might be very, very ill. This blanket use of agricultural antibiotics is thought to be blunting the effectiveness of these drugs on humans. And if antibiotics stop working on humans, then we might all start dying from infections again.

Well, that doesn't sound great. No, it doesn't. But Karro – which bills itself as one of the leading pork processors in the UK – has just registered an "antibiotic-free" trademark with the Intellectual Property Office.

What does that mean? It means that some meat will soon come packaged with a picture of a smiling pig, which will show that the animal wasn't treated with antimicrobial agents during its lifetime.

What a good idea! It's good, but not exactly new. Sweden banned agricultural antibiotics in 1986, and Denmark has cut down drastically in the last 20 years.

Does that mean that I can eat Danish bacon without worrying about getting MRSA? Probably, although don't forget the World Health Organisation's claim last year that bacon gives you cancer.

Actually, I've lost my appetite. I'm worried that this has been too preachy. Has it been too preachy?

A bit. Sorry. Eat what you like, I say. We've all got to die of something, right?

Do say: "Finally, meat you can eat with a clear conscience."

Don't say: "So long as you're cool with the mass murder of millions of animals, obviously."

~ KING HENRY 1 ~

Age: 948.

Appearance: Squashed underneath a car park.

You must be thinking of Richard III. Are you accusing me of muddling my dead kings? Everyone knows that Henry I is 400 years older than Richard III.

But it was Richard III who they found in a car park, not Henry I. Let me put this to you: what if they were both buried in car parks?

Surely not. It's looking likely. Archaeologists have just started exploring the area surrounding the ruined Reading Abbey, which is thought to contain Henry's remains.

They paved the abbey and put up a parking lot? Worse. They built a school on the abbey, and put a car park next to it, and that's where Henry is likely to be buried.

This sounds very specific for a brand-new archeological dig. Well, in truth, people already have a good idea of where he is. Records show that he was buried in front of the high altar, and calculations based on the size of the abbey appear to put him underneath the school car park.

A fitting location for a king who loved children. Henry I is famous for allowing his two granddaughters to be mutilated – they were blinded and their noses were cut off – in order to settle a political squabble.

Yeesh. Yeah. Probably not a bad thing to move him out of there, really.

Still, what a boon for Reading! If they find his remains, it will be just like when Leicester found Richard III. There will be TV shows about it, an inexplicable uplift in the fortunes of the local football team and a special Kasabian concert.

God, really? Well maybe not Kasabian, but Reading FC just appointed a manager people have heard of.

Still, car parks are getting quite de rigueur for dead kings, aren't they? Indeed. De rigueur mortis, you might say.

I hate you. I'm just saying, one dead king in a car park is a fluke. Two dead kings seems deliberate. Do we know where Henry VIII is? Shall we exhume the Chatham Aldi car park just in case?

Do say: "Can all these kings stop getting buried in car parks?"

Don't say: "Next week, we find Æthelred the Unready near some bins in Carlisle."

13/06/2016

~ JACK WILLS ~

Age: 17.

Appearance: Offensively sexy.

Jack Wills the brand? That's it. Aimed at students. Pheasant with a walking stick for a logo. Quite posh.

And that's sexy? Well, no, the brand isn't sexy. The brand sells expensive hoodies and overpriced polo shirts. It sells a boating blazer so obnoxious that it must exist only to help identify people who want to be punched. Jack Wills isn't sexy.

Then what is? A recent Jack Wills mailout catalogue. It was so sexy it ended up banned.

What's so sexy about it? It contains images of several attractive teenagers standing around in their pants, having fun.

I hate stupid sexy fun. Me too. Imagine seeing a catalogue like that as a kid and realising that you would one day be expected to stand around in your pants with your friends in an annoyingly louche manner. It would ruin your life.

Oh God, were these catalogues addressed to children? That's appalling. Well, no. They were actually addressed to adults. But one of the adults was a parent, and that parent had kids who might feasibly have seen the catalogue, so they complained. Does that count?

I don't think so. Well, the Advertising Standards Authority said it did. Its statement read: "The images in question showed [teenagers] relaxing and engaging in activities such as dancing, drinking and reading a newspaper together."

Teenagers reading a newspaper? What an obscene fantasy! The ASA goes on: "Moreover, we noted that the story of the group of friends depicted them dancing and drinking while fully clothed, then dancing and drinking in their underwear ... and a final scene of all of the characters in their underwear in bed together. We considered that this sequence of images ... was sexually suggestive."

And so it has been banned? Absolutely. Presumably, all future Jack Wills catalogues will feature normal teenage activities, such as being spotty and playing Xbox and having bad hair.

But where will kids find pictures of nudity now? Nowhere. The images were only available in that one Jack Wills catalogue, and now it has been banned. Our kids are safe again! Thanks, ASA!

Do say: "Jack Wills: Fabulously British."

Don't say: "Jack Wills: Perverted Newspaper-promoting Fetishists." 01/06/2016

~ MIPSTERS ~

Age: Between 16 and 24.

Appearance: Like hipsters, but Muslim.

That's what a mipster is? A Muslim hipster? Yes.

Is that allowed? Why wouldn't it be?

I don't know. I'm afraid to ask any more questions. Actually mipsters are only a sub-type – they're a sort of gummy.

Gummy? What's a gummy? A global, urban Muslim.

Is someone in charge of making up these words? Are there any rules at all? Mipster was originally coined on an American listserv for young Muslims who strove to combine Islam with a modern urban lifestyle, although in that case the plural was rendered Mipsterz.

Why must a modern urban lifestyle have to be incompatible with good spelling? These days words like gummy and mipster are more often deployed as marketing terms. Gummies, for example, represent an emergent category of consumer – "hyperdiverse, spiritual rather than religious-with-a-capital-R, educated, transnational".

And mipsters? They're the young, hip end of gummiedom, sometimes known as Generation M. Their hallmarks are identity, fashion, friendship and education.

What does that even mean? I don't know, but it's important to keep tabs on what young Muslims get up to these days, so we can target them more effectively.

You sounded a bit like Donald Trump just then. Not at all. We just need to learn as much about mipsters as possible.

Why? So we can sell them more stuff. According to the Muslim Lifestyle Expo conference, Muslims are a huge and largely untapped commercial market.

Are you saying Muslims don't shop? Of course they do – the worldwide market for halal products is worth £1.5 trillion annually.

Whoa. But mipsters' needs still aren't being addressed effectively at retail level. There are missed opportunities in the travel sector, skincare, fashion and lifestyle brands.

There were those burkinis you could buy at M&S. True, but at the moment big companies are losing out to startups created by young, entrepreneurial Muslims who've spotted the gap in the market.

Mipsters are doing it for themselves? If you like.

Do say: "Young Muslims have demonstrated their increasing power. We have to make a bigger effort to understand their changing cultural requirements …"

Don't say: "…so we can sell them well-sick hijabz."

10/06/2016

~ BEES ~

Age: Their earliest known ancestor was fossilised in the Cretaceous period.

Appearance: 20,000 different species exist, but they've generally all got the stripey, yellow'n'black bee-ish thing going on.

I know what this is about! Colony-collapse disorder! It is potentially the single greatest environmental catastrophe to befall us. The bees are dying! The number of native UK species has already halved. If the bees go, we all go. No more pollination means massive crop failure, mass starvation and death. SAVE THE BEES. No, they're Gwyneth Paltrow's new beauty aid.

Pass Notes

What? They're Gwyneth Paltrow's new beauty aid.

I see. Yes.

Go on, then. Tell me what new way we have found to press the precious resources of our natural world into the service of celebrity. In brief: you let them sting you, and the venom ...

Yes? I dunno ... makes you healthy, keeps you looking young, reduces your cholesterol, pays off your mortgage, makes you see stars and unicorns? Something like that. It's called apitherapy.

I have never met an apitherapist. I think they're all in LA. They claim bee stings are good for relieving arthritis, treating multiple sclerosis and cervical cancer and as a natural alternative to antibiotics.

I ain't letting nothing sting me on the cervix. I hear you.

Why would people believe such a thing? Beats me. Natural gullibility? Desperation? Stupidity? The death of God? Take your pick.

Don't bees die when they've stung you? Some do – leaving the stinger behind also pulls out part of their guts, which does not make for a long or happy life thereafter. I'm going to assume apitherapists use ones for whom plumping a star's epidermis does not require mortal wounding.

Gwyneth Paltrow moves in a world that advocates vaginal steaming. I would put nothing past her. I know. I know.

Shouldn't we be outlawing all frivolous bee use until we have figured out this whole planet-threatening, mass-death thing? Like we had to melt down railings and ornaments in the war to make bombs and things. You would think so, wouldn't you? But apparently we would rather look 25 and die than wrinkle and live.

Do say: "This bee totally ridiculous."

Don't say: "Oh, let her bee."

05/06/2016

~ JUICERO ~

Age: New!

Appearance: A sort of white thing.

Is this a juicer? Duh, I mean yeah, if you think a Ferrari is "a car".

Well it is. Never mind that. Juicero is a WiFi-enabled juicing system, app and chopped-fruit-and-vegetable delivery service that has just launched in California.

So it's like every buzzy startup idea ever, all rolled into one? That's right, which is probably why the founder, a juicevangelist called Doug Evans, has managed to raise $120m (£84m) in investments from companies such as Google and Campbell's Soup.

What the… ! $120m for a product that hasn't even launched yet? I know. And each Juicero machine is priced at $699 (£490), with each pouch of fruit and veg costing between $5 and $7.

Who on earth would be willing to pay that much for a juicer that commits them to spending a fiver each time they make a glass of juice? Gwyneth Paltrow loves it, apparently.

Of course she does. How about anyone non-rich? We're about to find out. "Juicero makes it easy to get your nutritious dose of fresh, raw, organic fruits and vegetables," the company explains.

I didn't realise it was hard. Don't you just buy some and eat them? I suppose you might.

Or you could buy cartons of juice, or get one of those Nutribullet blenders that people seem to like? I suppose. But who has time to actually buy and rinse things? Instead, with Juicero, you just take a packet of sealed ingredients out of the fridge and hang it in your machine, which reads a QR code on the back, determines that it's fresh, and squeezes it incredibly hard, sending all the juice into a glass below. Then you just chuck the pack into landfill – or cut it open with scissors, scrape out the old pulp, rinse it clean, and put it in the recycling.

I see ... So it's like mindbendingly expensive coffee pods for juice, then? Almost exactly like that, yes. Venture capitalists expect it to "disrupt" the home-juicing market.

Do what to the what, now? Make people unhappy with the juicers they already have.

Ah. Except the crackpots who actually eat fruit and vegetables? They won't care, right? Yeah. Those weirdos are in a world of their own.

Do say: "Think of us as your personal juicing sous chef."

Don't say: "Think of us when we go bust."

~ GHOSTING ~

Age: The word – new-ish, the concept – ageless.

Appearance: Immaterial. Geddit?

Ah, wait, I know this one! Is it clean eating until you look like a ghost? Or die of boredom and actually become a ghost? No. It's when you're going out with someone and then you just … don't, any more. You stop returning calls, texts, emails and basically unilaterally absent yourself from the relationship. Which is now no relationship. Because you're not there. Like a ghost. A cruel, cowardly, morally repugnant ghost.

That's scarier than any ghoulish phantom. I know. And, apparently, nearly 80% of millennials have experienced it.

Yikes! 80%? What is WRONG with the world? Is nobody good any more? Is nobody kind? Is nobody upstanding, compassionate, less than wholly, irredeemably selfish? No. Swipe left.

It must indeed be a Tinder-y, Snapchatty modern phenomenon. I mean, in this digital age, aren't we all just pixellated shadows of ourselves anyway? Why not ghost when you have no real connection? When we are all just phantasmagoria in the Cloud? It's a brutal, disassociated world out there all right. Though you can also "ghost" more positively.

How so? It also refers to leaving a party without saying goodbye.

I've been doing that for years. No one has noticed yet. I should probably make more of an effort at parties. It's also known as the Irish goodbye and the French exit.

I am neither Gaelic nor Gallic. I just can't be arsed. Some people do it because it saves the host being interrupted a million times by people bidding farewell. The party can keep running smoothly.

That's nice. I do it because I suddenly become so overwhelmed by the fact that I'm out, with people infinitely more capable of having fun than I, and music, and talking, and noise and people that I have to go before I kill. You're a spectre at the feast before you ghost. Respect.

Do say: "Thank you for this gift of sexual congress. I do not wish to take our relationship further, but I wish you well in all your future endeavours."

Don't say: "…"

29/06/2016

~ BLONDES ~

Age: About 11,000 years old, genetically.

Appearance: Just fabulous!

There you go, perpetuating the dumb-blond stereotype! I thought Reese Witherspoon had dealt with this in that civil rights documentary? Legally Blonde?

That's the one. I don't think that was a documentary. Besides, I'm not here to perpetuate anything. Rather the opposite in fact, because new research in the US suggests that naturally blond women are no dumber than anybody else. Indeed, they may be cleverer in some ways.

Woo-hoo! In your face, non-blondes! Let me feast on the details. Well, the study used old data from a long-running national survey conducted regularly on 10,878 ordinary

Americans who were aged 14–22 in 1979.

OK. Participants were given a kind of intelligence test, and at one point were also asked their natural hair colour. Based on this data, after various statistical adjustments, blond and brown-haired white women, on average, had an IQ a couple of points higher than white women with red or black hair.

Yeah! Blond and brown-haired women were also quite a bit more likely to be at the "genius level", with an IQ of more than 125.

Kiss my underpigmentation! Except …

Oh, here we go. Except, there are rather a lot of problems when you look deeper. For one thing, more than 93% of all white women said they had either blond or brown hair, so it is hardly a distinction to be one of them. The data on the other women looks a bit shaky too, since it's based on just 195 answers.

Right. Also, there seem to be more blond women than blond men in the survey, which there shouldn't be, so bleach or wishful thinking have probably interfered there.

Fine. In any case, general intelligence is a very slippery thing to measure, as it may well be influenced a lot by how you are brought up. For instance, as the study points out, the big survey also shows: "White, blond women grew up in homes with more reading material than those with other hair colour." And indeed, according to this survey, men generally are cleverer than women.

Oh, well, clearly it's a load of nonsense then. I think I agree.

Do say: "According to this dataset, blondes have 2.63% more fun."

Don't say: "Clearly, blond people should rule the world. Has anyone ever tried that?"

17/08/2010

~ SEX DUST ~

Appearance: A little brown jar filled with 2oz/56g of powder.

Available from: Gwyneth Paltrow's goop.com.

Price: $60/£42.50

That's a lot of money for not very much powder. What does it do? Well, it calls itself an "aphrodisiac warming potion".

Sounds good! How does it work? Basically you dissolve some in a drink. Then the dust "is designed to stimulate and cultivate sexual flow in both men and women … send sensitivity and power to all the right places, supporting primordial energy and vital essence".

Fantastic! Just a couple of quick questions before we begin our three-day bonk binge. What actually are "sexual flow", "primordial energy" and "vital essence"? Oh, they're just some deeply scientific things that the manufacturer, Gwyneth's friend Amanda Chantal Bacon, likes to talk about.

Right. And people will spend $60 on this stuff, will they? It seems so. Sex Dust is currently out of stock on Goop, even though a lecturer in human nutrition at Reading University describes himself as "rather sceptical" about its efficacy. "The products throw a lot of Chinese medicinal products together for which the evidence is primarily anecdotal," Dr Danny Commane told wired.co.uk, after casting an eye over other Moon Juice products.

And Moon Juice is? It's Bacon's very funny company, "a cosmic beacon for those seeking out beauty, wellness and longevity" which sells "miraculous lifestyle tools" to rich people in California. This week Moon Juice recommends that you build an actual shrine to their products. "Create a simple altar to honour them out in the open," it says, "to encourage sprinkling, nibbling and blending with whimsy of the spices, herbs and petals".

Surely they also provide a good evidence-base for their claims? Not really. To be fair, it's hard to give an evidence-base for statements such as: "I like to think of Moon Juice as an etheric potion that is coming from the cosmos to save the entire human race."

Yes. The closest they get is a mention of Bacon's own "transformative experience – backed up by extensive blood tests, the scrutiny of several physicians, renewed feelings of vitality, and a shift in my personality, immunity, appearance and thought".

I think we'd all get renewed feelings of vitality if we could shift 2oz of dust at 40 quid a time! I think so, too.

Do say: "There's one hypno-birthed every minute."

Don't say: "Is that why the NHS still spends millions on homeopathy?"

16/03/2016

~ ! ~

Pronunciation: "Exclamation mark" or, if you're a fan of Californian dance-punk bands, "Chk".

Appearance: Overused, apparently!

OK, calm down. You calm down! I'm perfectly calm! This is just how I happen to talk!

You don't seem particularly calm. Well, fine! If you must ask, I'm a bit put out by a new government directive regarding punctuation at primary-school level!

Why, what has happened? New guidance for Key Stage 1 and 2 National Curriculum tests has stated that pupils should only get credit if they use exclamation marks in sentences that begin with the words "What" or "How"!

Really? Yes! "A sentence that ends in an exclamation mark, but which does not have one of the grammatical patterns shown above is not considered to be creditworthy as an exclamation (eg exclamatory statements, exclamatory imperatives, exclamatory interrogatives or interjections)," it says!

That's probably a good thing, though. What? No! No it isn't! Exclamation marks are brilliant!

Only in moderation. Rely on them too much and you run the risk of sounding like an over-caffeinated toddler. Nonsense! Exclamation marks are the best! Everyone knows that! This guidance is effectively proof that the government wants to penalise enthusiasm! It's a disaster! A disaster!!

Are you ... no, actually, never mind. No! Finish your sentence! I demand it!

I don't quite know how to put this, but are you Kanye

West? Yes!!!! I'm Kanye West! Happy now? You're having a conversation with Kanye West!! Without exclamation marks, I'd be nothing! I'd just be a subdued egotist! And that's the worst kind of egotist!!

Look, Kanye, calm down. I'm sure there's a workaround here. I don't know what you mean! Tell me what you mean!

Well, for example, has the government issued a similar diktat about interrobangs? Interrobangs!? I don't think so!?!

Perhaps we could punish the government by teaching the nation's seven-year-olds to use those instead. YES!? LET'S COMPENSATE WITH INTERROBANGS!? AND ONLY EVER USING UPPERCASE TEXT?! THIS IS AMAZING!?!?! EAT IT, THE GOVERNMENT?!?!?!?!

Do say: "Remember, children, you'll be awarded zero credit for writing: 'I hate the government!' Instead, try writing: 'What a pointless nimrod the education secretary is!'"

Don't say: "Let's teach kids to emphasise with emojis instead."

07/03/2016

~ MISERDEN, GLOUCESTERSHIRE ~

Age: Old enough to be mentioned in the Domesday Book – which was completed in 1086 – under its former name, Greenhampstead.

Appearance: The living embodiment of nominative determinism.

I can't remember what nominative determinism is. Let me Google that. Hold up a second. Before you Google anything, do you live in Miserden?

I do, yes. Then don't bother Googling anything. Walk to a library and look it up instead. It'll be so much quicker, I promise.

But the nearest library is four miles away. It'll take me 90 minutes to walk there. Listen to me. It'll still be quicker.

Why's that? Because Miserden has officially the UK's stingiest broadband download speeds, that's why. Tests have shown that the local population endures an average speed of 1.3Mbps. One especially unlucky resident there even recorded a speed of 0.12Mbps.

Is that slow? Given that the average speed in the UK is 22.8Mbps, it's incredibly slow. It would take you about 11 hours to download a film. That's literally almost twice as long as it would take on Mount Everest.

That doesn't seem fair. It's not. Although Miserden is the worst, there are several of these rural blackspots around the country. The risk is that everyone will eventually move out of these areas, because they won't be able to email their family or watch that YouTube video of the sneezing panda.

Oi, spoilers! I've been trying to download that video for the past three hours! Have you got to the bit where the panda looks as if it's about to sneeze?

No. See what a mess this is? Most of the country takes reliable, high-speed internet for granted, and basic neglect like this risks turning some of our prettiest villages into ghost towns.

It's OK. We persevere. Wait a minute, are you reading this online?

I am, yes. When are you reading this?

Well, I started loading the page the second it was published, so it's now October 2018. Oh, wow, you're from the future. Say hello to President Trump for me!

Do say: "Access to the internet is a fundamental human right."

Don't say: "How am I going to get all my cat gifs now? Go outside and look at a cat? Yuck."

06/03/2016

~ FEBRUARY 29TH ~

Age: Four times younger than every other date.

Appearance: Hands down the worst day of the year.

The worst day? But it's magical. No, it isn't. 29th February is a dirty, capitalist day, geared purely towards the needs of the 1%.

But it's the date when women get to propose to men. Oh, big whoop. Listen, women can do what they want when they want. But, hey, well done for reinforcing the patriarchy, 29th February. Great job.

What if you're born on 29th February? Doesn't that make

you special? Only special in the sense that Facebook always messes up your birthday. It has no way of telling whether you celebrate your non-leap-year birthdays on 28th February or 1st March, which means it often gets it wrong.

Can we go back a bit? Why is 29th February capitalist? Let me ask you a question. Are you on a salary?

Yes. And that salary is based on the assumption that you work full-time over a 365-day year?

That's right. Well, there are 366 days this year. Today, you're basically working for free.

What? That's an outrage! I know! We should all down tools, right this minute. If our greedy corporate overlords valued us in the slightest, they'd give us an extra day's pay. Right now. In an envelope.

Actually, they should give me two envelopes, because I'm writing both sides of this conversation. It gets worse. Banks don't usually count 29th February when they work out customer interest. Today, the banks keep back your hard-earned money as profit.

That's disgusting. Something should be done. It's terrible. Roll on the year 2100, I say.

Why? Isn't that a leap year, too? No, because years divisible by 100 aren't leap years. February 2100 will only have 28 days.

But 2000 was a year divisible by 100, and that was a leap year. Yes, but only because 2000 is also divisible by 400, which negates the previous "divisible by 100" rule.

I'm so confused. See? This is exactly what the corporations want. To rule by obfuscation. They're bleeding us dry. We're all doomed.

Do say: "Occupy 29th February!"

Don't say: "Actually, I'm freelance, so none of this means anything to me."

29/02/2016

~ MR AND MRS AMAZING ~

Name: Mr and Mrs Amazing.

Age: Unknown.

Appearance: Officially Amazing.

Are they married superheroes? Possibly, but unlikely.

How did they come by such an unusual and hard-to-live-up-to surname? They paid for it.

Who did they buy it from? No one. The Amazings are just two of the 85,000 people who legally changed their names by deed poll last year.

They're being silly, then. Not as silly as the man who changed his name to Bacon Double Cheeseburger.

Why did he do that? "Bacon Double Cheeseburger was the first name I came up with," he said.

What could he possibly have been called for before, that he felt Bacon Double Cheeseburger constituted an improvement? He was called Simon.

Fair play to him. What other monikers have people have chosen? Bruce Wayne, Penelope Pitstop, Cristiano Ronaldo, Sarge Metalfatigue and Happy Birthday, to name but a few.

It sounds to me as if this procedure isn't expensive enough. Actually, it doesn't cost anything. You can even make your own form. But if you want your deed poll enrolled with the courts, it costs £36.

What if I decide I don't like my new name? You can change it as many times as you like, for any reason besides fraud.

Are there no rules at all? Names such as Jesus and Satan are forbidden, because they're blasphemous. And first names can't be anything that is also a rank or title, such as Sir, Lord, Duke, Professor or Doctor.

That's all my best ideas gone. I might change my name to "password123", so I only have one thing to remember. Sorry, no numbers or symbols are allowed. And surnames are limited to 50 characters.

What are some non-stupid reasons for changing your name? You might want a new identity to go with your new gender, or so you can hide from an abusive partner. Last year, a student changed his name by deed poll because it was cheaper than getting Ryanair to alter the name on his ticket.

Do say: "Next door's bins are in our front garden again. Bloody Amazings."

Don't say: "We don't serve Bacon Double Cheeseburgers here. This is Starbucks. Now tell me your name so I can write it on the cup.

22/02/2016

~ EMMA THOMPSON ~

Age: 56.

Appearance: Emma Thompson!

Ah, Emma Thompson ... Who doesn't love Emma Thompson? The *Sun,* the *Mail,* Stewart Jackson MP, Steve Baker MP, James Cleverley MP, Jacob Rees-Mogg MP, Conor Burns MP, Daniel Hannan MEP, former MEP Godfrey Bloom ...

Ah. Is this about that thing she said? It is. She was in Berlin promoting her new film and said she would vote to stay in the EU, calling Britain "a tiny little cloud-bolted, rainy corner of sort-of Europe, a cake-filled, misery-laden, grey old island".

What a splendid turn of phrase she has. How neatly that captures the British spirit of tender self-deprecation. Yeah, about that. The *Sun* has responded by superimposing a slice of Victoria sponge on a picture of her face and put it on the cover with the headline: "Shut yer cakehole!"

They don't like tender self-deprecation? That's not really their thing, no. They also call her a "pro-EU super-luvvie".

Sounds fair. Many of the MPs were rather meaner. "Ms Thompson is typical of the worst sort of fat-cat luvvie," Burns said. "Most Brits love Britain and will see the referendum as a celebration of democracy our ancestors died to defend. Sadly, they also died to allow snooty ladies like Ms Thompson to vent their metropolitan elitist snobbery."

Wait a minute. Is she against democracy, too? No, that's just some word-twisting on Burns's part. I think he's confusing her with Isis, Hitler, etc.

Easily done. So, basically, he's saying she's entitled to her opinion? Yes, kind of. Bloom volunteered to "spank her silly bottom".

I bet he did. Unfortunately, no ancestors died for that. Hannan brings up a technical issue with her. "In what sense is Britain a 'tiny little island', Emma Thompson?" he asked. "Geography? Economics? Diplomatic reach?"

Well? It's geography. He was right the first time. Within Europe, the island of Great Britain is smaller than France, Spain, Sweden, Norway, Germany, Finland, Poland, Italy and Romania.

Still, you shouldn't admit that in front of a bunch of Germans, should you? No. That's our little secret.

Do say: "I'm pretty sure our ancestors died so that Europeans would stop fighting each other."

Don't say: "And to defend the British empire, which was – ahem! – far from democratic."

17/02/2016

~ CIRCUMFLEX ~

Nom: Circumflex, or in French, *circonflexe*.

Quel âge a-t-il? Oh, it goes back thousands of years, to ancient Greece.

Apparence: Like a lovely little sunhat. It's a diacritic that sits on top of letters in many modern languages, although most famously in French.

Et les Français? Pourquoi do they it use? Oh, it's just part of how they write some words, to denote a vanished letter, usually an "s".

Pourquoi need-they un diacritique special pour telling tout le monde que il y a un "s" disparu? Well, occasionally it helps distinguish between different words, such as *cote* (meaning level) and *côte* (meaning coast), but most of the time it just hangs around on words such as *être*, looking cool, but not really doing much.

Un peu comme les Français eux-selves? You might say that about our dear neighbours and allies. I couldn't possibly comment. Although, as it happens, the Académie Française agrees with you, at least about the circumflex.

L'académie Française! Les world-famous ultra-fogeys qui détestent le franglais? I'm not sure they would agree with the description, but, yes, them. They have issued a list of approved alternatives to some written French words, which have removed a lot of hyphens and the circumflex on such words as *coût* and *paraître*.

Mon dieu! Yes, that's how France has reacted.

When ont-ils issued ces alternatives? Well, that's the thing.

In 1990.

Vingt-six years ago? Yes.

So pourquoi le brouhaha now? It seems that French publishers are as speedy as French bureaucrats, because they only updated the school textbooks this year. That was duly noticed by the TV station TF1, then social media got involved ... then student groups and politicians ...

Mais, changing la langue française! C'est un big deal, n'est-ce pas? Not very big in this case. Remember, these are only approved alternatives. Where the circumflex on an "i" or "u" has no effect on meaning, it is no longer obligatory, but no one will be marked wrong for continuing to use it.

So les Français ont overreacté to un very petit adjustment à leur way of life? That's right.

Typique! Yes. No one ever overreacts to things over here.

Dire: "How could they ban a harmless little hat?"

Ne pas dire: "Well, they banned the veil."

05/02/2016

~ GOSSIP BOMB ~

Age: Nuovo.

Appearance: Naughty.

Go on then, tell me which hip young groovebag has come up with this new phrase. PewDiePie? Zoella? Pope Francis.

Eh? Was he at least pronouncing a sick burn on Instagram or something? He was giving an improvised speech on clerical discipline to thousands of priests in the Vatican.

Yeah, that's not quite the same. So what is a "gossip bomb"? Hard to say exactly. The Holy Father was explaining how Jesus wants priests to do what the church authorities tell them, without being all awkward and questiony. As their numbers fall dramatically, they must also stick together, he said, and not divide communities by spreading gossip.

Yeah, because if the Catholic church has learned anything in the past few years, it is that priests must keep quiet when they hear about anything dodgy. Quite. Anyway, the pope then illustrated his point by saying that gossips are like terrorists setting off bombs in their communities. "If you get an urge to say something against a brother or a sister, to drop a gossip bomb, bite your tongue," he said. "Hard!"

Ow! Not you. You're not a consecrated priest or nun in the Catholic church. You can gossip about whoever you like, as long as we can get it past the lawyers.

Thanks. Do you think maybe the pope was thinking of photobombs, the F-bomb and suchlike? It's possible. These are just the kind of 21st-century phrases you would expect from a groovy, modern, 79-year-old celibate religious conservative. After all, he has released a rock album, he is going to be in a film, he gets tons of retweets …

Sorry, did you say the pope is going to be in a film? That's right.

What kind of film? It's called Beyond the Sun, and it is "a family adventure based on the Gospels".

Taking an ambivalent, critically engaged look at the Gospels? Probably more of a completely-believing-them one. It is being co-financed by the rum heiress Monika Bacardi. The pope plays himself.

So maybe his whole career to date, maybe even this speech, was method acting? Maybe.

Do say: "And don't drop the contraception bomb either."

Don't say: The Galileo bomb is now tolerated.

02/02/2016

~ THE EMPIRE ~

Age: More than 400 years old.

Appearance: Pink.

Ooh, what's up? Is it striking back again? No.

Are the Siths coming? Or going? I've lost track. Bring me my Star Wars box set. No, not that empire. The British empire.

The wha'? The British empire.

Oh, that. The sun-never-set one? Exactly. A fifth of the world's population were governed by us at our 1922 peak, over a quarter of the world's terra firma.

Thesubjugating-of-uncountable-millions-pillaging-of-their-lands-and-suffering-visited-upon-generations one? That's an extremely fusty and old-fashioned view.

It's really not. It really is, you know. A YouGov poll held ahead of Tuesday's Oxford Union debate about removing the statue of Cecil Rhodes from outside Oriel College showed that 43% of British people thought that the empire was a good thing.

Were all those polled from inside Oriel College? No. And 44% thought that Britain's history of colonialism was something we should be proud of.

Groping desperately for specks of hope in the mire of despair, I say that still leaves a majority saying it's something we should regret. No, only 21% said that; 23% said "neither" and the rest either didn't know or wouldn't say.

So, basically, nearly half the population thinks the Amritsar massacre, the concentration camps during the Boer war and after the Mau Mau uprising, the post-partition violence in India caused by uprooting 10 million people, and the four million deaths from famine in Bengal while Churchill diverted grain to British troops and other countries were – what? Dunno. Not things they knew about? The price of doing business? We did bring a lot of economic development to places, you know.

I'm sure the bones of starving children thank you. Anyway, Churchill was wonderful in the war.

Was he? "I hate Indians," he said, talking about the Bengal famine in 1943. "They are a beastly people with a beastly religion. The famine was their own fault for

breeding like rabbits." Um … all great men have their blind spots?

Is that honestly the best defence you have? That and this poll. Can 44% of random punters really be wrong?

Yes. Well, I mean, when you put it that way, yes, you're obviously right.

Do say: "You ought to be ashamed of yourselves!"

Don't say: "But without it, we would all have to learn foreign!"

20/02/2016

~ PEAK CURTAINS ~

Appearance: Cluttered.

Oh God, not another peak something … This isn't just peak something, this is peak everything.

I thought you said it was peak curtains? That was kind of a metonym.

What's a metonym? It's when a bit of something stands for all of it. Curtains are just one example of all the stuff that Ikea's head of sustainability Steve Howard reckons people in the developed world can't buy any more of.

Ikea's head of sustainability? Yes. He was speaking at a *Guardian* Sustainable Business debate.

Sounds like something he would do. "We talk about peak oil," he said. "I'd say we've hit peak red meat, peak sugar, peak stuff … peak home furnishings." Later he settled on the snappier "peak curtains".

Good call. So no one is ever going to buy another pair of curtains, is that what he's saying? I don't think so. He means that people just can't consume stuff any faster than they do already.

I wouldn't bet on that. I love consuming. You buy a £30 lamp thinking it will make you happy, and it does for about 20 minutes, then you kind of forget about it, then you start to worry that life is meaningless, then you buy another lamp. Why tinker with a perfect formula? Because the ecosystem can't take it. If we keep going, the world will become so inhospitable, and resources so scarce, that we'll end up having massive wars over what is left.

OK. Maybe do tinker a bit. That is Howard's plan. "We will be increasingly building a circular Ikea where you can repair and recycle products," he says.

Doesn't the current Ikea make billions by producing vast quantities of disposable cheap tat? €30bn worth of disposable cheap tat in 2014, to be precise, yes. But now it is trying to mend its ways.

By making vague promises at *Guardian* events? Absolutely. And by replacing all its lights with LEDs, spending 2.1bn since 2009 to make stores run entirely on renewable power by 2020 and by donating €400m to mitigate climate change in the places worst affected.

But in future I'll have to repair my lamp instead of buying a new one? I'm afraid so. Try getting a nice lamp to start with.

Do say: "If only it were somehow possible to buy secondhand furniture …"

Don't say: "Do you think these curtains are a bit 2005?

18/06/2016"

~ THE NAUGHTY PAUSE ~

Age: The term is new, but the practice is in fact as old as time.

Appearance: Almost cartoonishly French.

Really? Is this about shrugging? No. Have you ever heard of *le cinq à sept?*

I have not. Well, brace yourself – it's the French term for having it off in the afternoon.

In the afternoon? What a disgrace. Well, let's not judge. *Cinq à sept* are the hours when a philanderer will book a hotel for a quickie, before returning home to their oblivious family.

That'll never catch on in Britain. We like to have sex the traditional way. Quiet, with the lights out, with our spouse, for 45 seconds, one night a month. *Au contraire!*

We're not! We are! Only over here we're calling it "the naughty pause", because *le cinq à sept* is in French, and the only French anyone can remember is for "Where is the swimming pool?", "I have two sisters and a brother", and "I am 11 years old".

Who decided to call it the naughty pause? Very possibly, a website that books out hotel rooms by the hour. Very possibly, because it needed a marketing gimmick to drum up custom.

Right, so it's all nonsense. Apparently not. The site claims to have experienced 150% growth for the past two years, and expects to have two million customers within five years.

Who knew we were so immoral? The bookings aren't all for affairs. Apparently, 40% of the site's clients are people who need a second office, and a further 20% are air passengers who require a quick nap.

That's a euphemism if ever I heard one. Well, that still leaves 40% of people who sign up for some afternoon/early evening delight.

Maybe the British are a bit French after all. We've still got some way to go. The French version of the site includes fairly indiscreet add-ons, such as champagne and something called a "lovebox", which probably aren't designed with napping air passengers in mind.

What does the British site offer in comparison? Not much yet. Maybe an all-compassing sensation of deep shame, and possibly chlamydia.

Do say: "Je voudrais réserver une chambre pour une sieste."

Don't say: "A quelle heure est le petit déjeuner?"

13/01/2016

~ BARRY HUMPHRIES ~

Age: 81.

Appearance: The hilarious, ironically offensive alter ego of Dame Edna Everage.

Are you sure you've got that the right way round? Pretty sure, yes. Dame Edna is the performer, and Barry Humphries is her wildly overcooked caricature of spluttering rightwing outrage.

I don't think that's right. Of course it's right. Haven't you read the interviews to promote his new radio show? They're a Borat-level masterclass of sustained satire, skewering the backwards attitudes of conservative blowhards who spend their lives railing against the perceived threat of political correctness. It's tremendous.

Really? What did he say? He called Caitlyn Jenner a "mutilated man" and a "publicity-seeking ratbag" for starters. Brilliant.

OK, what else? He asked the *Radio Times*, "Why do you think Downton Abbey is so popular in the States?" before answering: "Because there are no black people in it." Take that, conservatives!

Is that everything? He has also hilariously dismantled the idea of BBC bias by claiming that an unnamed producer asked him to balance out jokes about Jeremy Corbyn in a recent routine by adding jokes about David Cameron.

Are you sure these aren't just his own personal views? Oh, hardly. Dame Edna is one of the most perfect creations ever to spike the trend of empty celebrity. This new Barry Humphries character is simply doing the same thing, but aiming his laser at the outdated beliefs of tedious old men.

Last time I'll ask: are you absolutely positive that this is a gag, and not just the desperate ravings of someone who's clearly losing touch with the world? Absolutely. After all, he spoke about a Nazi friend of his, whose dying words were: "Zat Barry Humphries, ze Führer would have adored him." You don't invoke Hitler's name in a funny accent to praise your own work unless it's a joke, right?

Um ... Oh God, did he mean it? Was Barry Humphries being sincere? Is he really proud that Hitler would have liked his comedy?

Look, there's a chance. And the Caitlyn Jenner thing? Holy christ! The man's a monster!

Unless he was joking. Oh God! I'm so confused!

Do say: "Everyone is entitled to their opinions."

Don't say: "Unless those opinions are awful and demonstrably wrong."

05/01/2016

~ KISSING UNDER THE MISTLETOE ~

Age: About 150 years old.

Appearance: Increasingly rare.

Don't tell me. Because of climate change? No mistletoe, plus everyone is too paralysed with fear of the impending apocalypse to want to get the snogs in. For once, no. Nowt to do with terrifying, unseasonally warm weather and its intimations of doom.

What's happening, then? A new survey by the impeccably qualified and unimpeachable team of researchers at Morrisons supermarket – which is in no way manufacturing a story that then allows it to give away sprigs of mistletoe to customers as a sales gimmick, as they happen to be doing at the moment – says that while 62% of over-55s have been kissed under the mistletoe at Christmas, 75% of people under 35 have not.

They have in my office. I sprayed on extra Lynx and made sure of it. Yeeesss … you see, this is part of the problem.

What is? The tradition that says any woman standing under mistletoe can be kissed –

And will be dogged by bad luck if she refuses. Don't forget that part. I never do. It will seal the deal. You are a delight. Yes, there's that part too – but it all sits increasingly uncomfortably with modern mores.

Which are? That women get quite enough unwanted kisses in life without the encouragement of Victorian traditions and viscum album.

Now wait – no one said anything about introducing viscum album into the proceedings. Even I wouldn't go that far. No, that's the proper name for mistletoe.

Thank God. So, what's to be done? Well, mistletoe sales have been declining for the past 20 years, but growers say 2015 has yielded a bumper-berried crop. So maybe the time, as well as the plant, is ripe for a resurgence.

I'm up for that, if you know what I mean! Fnaar fnaar! You're the worst.

Do say: "Let's willingly and consensually kiss to preserve this vital part of our heritage, protect the mistletoe market and confer an air of lightly joyful but essentially innocent exuberance upon the gathering."

Don't say: "And let's use tongues."

21/12/2015

~ MORANBONG ~

Formed: July 2012.

Appearance: A large number of young North Korean women wearing quasi-military satin dress suits, each one holding a different musical instrument.

That sounds quite, um, formal. On the contrary, Moranbong are North Korea's first girl band, and a sign of how open the country has become to western popular influences. In their first concert, they wore ball gowns and minidresses and there were dancing Disney characters. Although, obviously, all that has now been toned down.

Obviously. And what is their music like? They are very skilled performers, on everything from violin and saxophone to drums and bass guitar, but I do suspect a bit of lip-syncing from the singers.

How about the songs? Oh, they're extremely bad – they even include covers of My Way and the Rocky theme. Kim Jong-un reportedly chooses the group members himself from the armed forces, and he does seem to be trying to move forward from the state orchestras of his father's day. However, the music sounds like a chatshow orchestra from the 1970s being told to fill time.

What are the songs about? The usual things. Mostly about how great North Korea is, or how happy its people are. Their biggest hits are We Like Centralisation and Our Families Won't Be Tortured If We Screw Up.

Really? No. But you get the gist. Anyway, Kim sent Moranbong on what was supposed to be their first foreign mission.

Shouldn't that be called a tour? If you prefer. They were scheduled to perform a series of shows at the National Centre for the Performing Arts in Beijing, along with the State Merited Chorus. But over the weekend the shows were abruptly cancelled and Moranbong returned to North Korea.

Oh. Well, who are the State Merited Chorus then? They're basically a musical battalion of the North Korean Army. Both camp and scary at the same time. They also cancelled.

Great. So did Chinese people actually want to listen to all this in the first place? Dunno. North Koreans love them. But the idea of the trip was more about improving relations with the Chinese government.

That obviously went well. So it'd have been a bit like when you go to your friend's house and they insist on playing you their favourite album really loud and you just have to sit there trying to look like you enjoy it? Yes. Except the friend has nuclear weapons.

Do sing: "If you want to be my lover, you've got to get approval from the interior ministry."

Don't sing: "Push the Button".

Also known as: Little Marx.

13/12/2015

~ JAR JAR BINKS ~

Age: Born in the year 52 BBY.

BBY? Before the Battle of Yavin, according to the Galactic Standard Calendar.

I see. Are you feeling OK? It might help if I mention that Jar Jar Binks is a Star Wars character.

Not really. I haven't seen a Star Wars film since the one with all the teddy bears. Binks first appeared in The Phantom Menace. He was also in the next two, Attack of the Clones and Revenge of the Sith.

What does he look like? An amphibious donkey after ill-advised collagen injections.

Think of the hours in makeup. Hardly any: Binks was a CGI concoction, a bumbling Gungan from the planet Naboo, brought in to provide comic relief.

So he was funny? No. He was irritating, with a silly voice and alien patois, which had enough of a Jamaican tinge to give rise to allegations (denied by creator George Lucas) of racist stereotyping. Binks is often considered the most hated character in the whole space saga, if not in the entire history of film.

He sounds ripe for rehabilitation, then. Not yet, it seems. At a press conference, producer Kathleen Kennedy said that Binks will not appear in the forthcoming Star Wars instalment, The Force Awakens.

How did she put it? "Jar Jar is definitely not in the movie."

Pretty unequivocal. Indeed. Her answer was greeted with cheers and applause.

So everybody's happy? Perhaps not everybody. For the last month or so a theory has been making the rounds among Star Wars fans, to the effect that goofy Binks is a powerful Sith lord in disguise – perhaps the Supreme Leader Snoke himself.

I don't know what that means, and I think I don't care. It's alleged that George Lucas had always intended for Binks to be revealed as a bad guy in later films, but lost his nerve when the character turned out to be so unpopular.

Thank you. Now I know I don't care. Some people even thought the director of the new film, JJ Abrams, might take the opportunity to re-establish Binks as a dark presence. But he hasn't.

What about the teddy bears? They're gone too.

Do say: "Jar Jar is dead. Long live JJ."

Don't say: "Yousa'll miss missa whena missa m gone."

07/12/2015

~ LSD ~

Full name: Lysergic acid diethylamide.

Age: First synthesised by Dr Albert Hoffman in Switzerland in 1938.

Appearance: Small squares of paper with pretty pictures on them.

Indications: When you want to laugh continuously for no reason for several hours while the walls melt and the carpet turns into almost like a sea of microscopic creatures. Also, when you have a tricky day ahead at work.

I don't think my square colleagues will approve of that. They're all, "Ooh, let's make a profit." "Let's fulfil our contractual obligations." "Please vomit somewhere else." That's quite common, but this is Californian business practice so the rest of the world will soon catch up.

Seriously? Taking acid at work? Yes. According to reports, LSD microdosing is now widespread in Silicon Valley offices.

Isn't it quite hard to debug software when your monitor is the mouth of a giant fish and all the code is just strands of flesh and seaweed caught in its teeth? Yes, that would be challenging, but this is microdosing – taking such a small amount of acid, or mushrooms, that the effect is only just noticeable and never becomes a full-blown trip. It's said to enhance energy and creativity, and LSD lacks the addictiveness and physical side effects of traditional performance-enhancing drugs such as speed or Ritalin.

Yeah. Traditional performance-enhancing drugs are so lame. CNN quotes a Cisco employee called Kevin Herbert. "There was a case where I had been working on a problem for over a month," Herbert said. "And I took LSD, and I just realised: 'Wait, the problem is in the hardware. It's not a software issue at all.'"

Far out. You may scoff, but quite a few computing pioneers were psychedelic drug users. Steve Jobs reportedly considered it one of the most important things he'd ever done.

I thought he was a massive control freak? Maybe the acid smoothed him out.

Do say: "Turn off, tune in. Turn on again."

Don't say: "By clicking 'Agree', you agree that you have read the terms and conditions and that everything in the universe is part of everything else on a level that human consciousness can't reach."

29/11/2015

~ NIGELLA LAWSON ~

Age: 55.

Appearance: Still the reigning queen of televised cookery.

Nigella's back! We haven't seen her on our screens since ... Since The Unpleasantness.

Oh yes, that business with Charles Saatchi. Well, actually I was referring to that rubbishy gameshow she did on Channel 4 a couple of years ago, but whatever.

Either way, hooray! What's the reason for her return? Because she loves us, and in her heart she knows that we've missed her.

Really? No, of course not. It's because she has a new book and television show out.

A new Nigella series? What's this one called? Its name is Simply Nigella.

I'm not exactly sure what that means. Then let me quote the book's official description for you. "Simply Nigella taps into the rhythms of our cooking lives, with recipes that are uncomplicated, relaxed and yet always satisfying."

So all the recipes are quick and easy? No, because her last book was the quick-and-easy book. That one was called Nigella Express, and its recipes were so quick and easy that one of them was literally just a load of Marmite tipped into a bowl of spaghetti and stirred around.

Yuck. Does that even count as a recipe? Probably not, but this is Nigella's world. We just happen to live in it.

Business as usual, then? Probably. The new show starts on Monday, so brace yourself for all the old Nigella favourites such as licked fingers, obliviously amused dinner party guests and thousands of steaming, unctuous, overflowing, blisteringly unnecessary adjectives.

Will these new episodes end in the traditional manner? With Nigella sneaking downstairs in her nightie, scooping up a handful of trifle from her fridge and shoving it in her mouth? They'd better. Imagine the outrage if they didn't.

So Nigella is back and Jamie Oliver is back. Does this mean that Gordon Ramsay will be back soon, too? Keep your voice down. The last thing anyone needs to do is give that man ideas.

Do say: "Coming up on BBC2: Simply Nigella."

Don't say: "Coming up on BBC2: Complicatedly Nigella, where she'll attempt to spin pasta from unicorn hair while tapdancing on the saddle of a flaming unicycle."

01/11/2015

~ HAY ON WYE ~

What is it? Bill Clinton's kinda town.

For the plentiful booze and chance of cigar-wielding fornication? Hardly. The remote Welsh border town of 1,300 has a bookshop for every 32 inhabitants, and its annual festival is, according to the former US president, 'the Woodstock of the mind'.

Did one of the town's 39 bookshop owners place empty cigar boxes and Ms Lewinsky's autobiography on display when Clinton visited? She did, but director Peter Florence prefers a 'festival of ideas' slant.

Is that why Ken Dodd spoke in 2001, Macy Gray performed in 2002 and disarmingly surly Irish bawler Van Morrison has favoured the Black Mountain town with a set this year? What if it is, chippy?

I ask the questions. How many *Guardian* people are there this year? One for every 32 visitors.

How many visitors are expected this year? At least 70,000.

So you're being silly then. Er, yes.

Which top literary turns are going to draw the crowds this year? Canadian poet turned dystopian visionary Margaret

Atwood spoke on Saturday, dystopian visionary Don DeLillo yesterday, and dystopian visionary turned funnyman Christopher Hitchens is due on tonight.

Run that one by me again. The bequiffed controversialist has a gig called Late Night Hitch. He's billed as "Lenny Bruce meets Wodehouse" and sponsored by Tyrells Potato Chips.

Ah. Anything in the Intellectual Rigour department? Edward Said, AC Grayling, Steve Jones, Eric Hobsbawm and Linda Colley.

What about Unscheduled Licking? Covered: Phil Nichol has done a show called *Things I Like I Lick,* featuring such-liked things as Travolta's legs, his hometown and his friend Sharon.

Do say: "The Richard Sennett lecture clashes with the Anthony Beevor talk. What is a thinking person to do?"

Don't say: "It's one o'clock. Let's go and heckle David Starkey.'

26/05/2003

~ THE AUSSIE BIBLE ~

"Abraham was told, Milcah has borne sons unto your brother Nahor: Uz his firstborn, then his brother Buz, and Kemuel father of Aram, and Kesed, Hazo, Pildash, Jidlaph and Bethuel; and ..." Jeez, mate, this is going on a bit.

Look, do you mind ... "These eight Milcah bore unto Abraham's brother Nahor. His concubine, whose name was Reumah, also bore him sons: Tebah, Gaham, Tahash ..." Strewth, this bloke's been busier than a cat burying shit.

Please be quiet! Alright, don't spit your dummy, sport.

"Abraham took unto himself another wife, Keturah ..." Isn't that on the Gold Coast, near Brisbane?

Oh, I give up. I take it you're Australian. Too right, mate – a citizen of Godzone.

Shame you have no appreciation of God – or the Bible. That's where you're wrong, mate. Us Aussies have got our own version now and about bloody time – the Aussie Bible. And best of all we've dropped Uz, Buz and all those other drongos. We're just concentrating on the important stuff.

And what, pray, do you consider the important stuff? The part where Mary pops a sprog in a feed trough, three wise guys show up with prezzies and the jackaroos roll into town for a squizz at the ankle-biter.

I think I prefer the glorious cadences of the King James's Version. It just wasn't playing in Ballarat, mate. Church attendances had gone down the dunny, so journo Kel Richards had the bright idea of doing the best bits in 'Strine.

'Strine? I take it you mean the argot of your country – carried across by convicts in the 19th century? Do you want a go, mate?

A go at what? I mean are you looking for a blue?

I haven't got a clue what you're on about. I'm going back to Genesis. Good move – great band, mate.

Don't recite: The First Book of Kings.

Do recite: The First Book of Kylie.

05/06/2003

~ CHRIS MARTIN ~

Unleash the groupies, dust off the bong, we're going on tour. It's gonna be wild, man! Trashing hotel rooms, illicit pharmaceuticals, different bird in every town. Rock'n'roll, man! Do you mind keeping it down a bit? Gwyneth and I are trying to do some yoga. We must have silence on the tour bus.

You got your main squeeze on the bus? Nightmare, man! What about coke? We gotta do some coke! Heavens, no. Gwyn's macrobiotic and I don't ingest anything stronger than cappuccinos. And only very milky ones.

But you're Chris Martin, Coldplay frontman, the sexual fantasy of a million oestrogen-charged, poetry-reading teenage girls. You should be exploiting your sexual allure in bouts of meaningless promiscuity with perfect strangers. Good point. I am, after all, the thinking girl's whiny geek. That said, I'm engaged to be married to Gwyneth Paltrow, the whiny geek's favourite pouting anglophile thesp. She'd rip off my cojones if I did anything like that.

Do you wuv her? Oh, yes. In fact, I've just written a new song as a testimony to our wuv.

If I pay you, will you refrain from singing it? No. Here it goes: "Come on now, don't you want to see?/ This thing that's happening to me/ Like Moses has power over sea/ So you've got power over me."

That's terrible. What's more, it was God not Moses who parted the Red Sea, brainiac. Hold on, I haven't finished. "And oh, oh, yes I would/ If only I could/ And you know I would/ And baby, oh baby I/ I wish/ I wish/ Oh, oh, oh/Oh, oh, oh."

I'd say it lost it towards the end, but it didn't have much to start off with.

Do say: "Come on now, don't you want to see?/Just what a difference you've made to me"

Don't say: "Gwyn! I got the munchies from all the drugs. Do us up a bacon toastie, babe."

26/03/2014

~ SEAMUS HEANEY ~

Now, I've heard of him. Of course you have. Not for nothing is he known as "Famous Seamus".

Who calls him that? Some grudging academics. All other poets.

Because of the Nobel Prize, that sort of thing? Indeed. He has pulled off the difficult trick of being a famous poet without being dead. Author of GCSE set texts, holder of any number of fellowships and professorships, the most recognisable poetic voice in the English-speaking world.

So, what has he famously done now? He told teenagers at the Prince of Wales Summer School in Norwich that the rapper Eminem is to be admired for his "verbal energy". He has "sent a voltage around a generation".

What features of Eminem's verse does he pinpoint? To tell the truth, he's rather vague. "There is this guy Eminem. He has created a sense of what is possible."

Do Heaney's words have anything in common with Eminem's? Heaney specialises in peat bogs, ancient history and rural labour. No mention of drugs, rape or trailer parks.

Mind you, his celebrated modernisation of *Beowulf* gets pretty nasty.

Typical Heaney lines? The cold smell of potato mould, the squelch and slap/ Of soggy peat, the curt cuts of an edge/ Through living roots.

Do say: "It takes one master bard to know another master bard."

Don't say: "Seamus, you're just as groovy as that Andrew Motion."

02/03/2003

~ GUINNESS ~

Age: In something like its current form, about 180 years. I mean, not your pint specifically – they don't usually take quite that long to pour.

Historical advertising message, abandoned under pressure from advertising authorities: Guinness is good for you.

More recent advertising message: Here are some horses galloping around in the sea. Drink Guinness!

Satisfyingly ironic discovery announced this week by researchers at the University of Wisconsin: Guinness is good for you. Comparatively.

Compared to what? Er, well, lager, to be fair. And lard. And stabbing yourself with a radioactive knife.

So, as with red wine and chocolate, what we thought was unhealthy turns out to be healthy? Just like red wine and chocolate. It's the flavonoids, you see – their preponderance in the black stuff means it works twice as well as lager at stimulating anti-clotting activity in the blood.

The Wisconsin scientists must be heartily sick of all those "call that work?" gags in the faculty common room. Oh, they didn't drink the Guinness themselves. They gave it to dogs.

What? They gave beer to dogs? Look, their parents were away, everyone was a bit stoned, and it just seemed kind of funny at the time. Plus, they needed a paper to present at this week's American Heart Association conference in Orlando, Florida.

Do: Drink about a pint, with food, in order to experience the greatest benefits, according to the study's lead researcher.

Don't: Drink about four pints, instead of food. Or drink any at all if you're on the Atkins diet. Then again...

Also don't: Go on the Atkins diet, because it's stupid.

Other papers coming soon from the Wisconsin team: Influence of Daily Mars Bar Intake on Resting, Working and Playing Activity Among Wisconsin Dogs; Is Coke It?: Preliminary Findings from the Wisconsin Dog Cohort.

14/11/2003

~ ANNA KARENINA ~

Occupation: Heroine.

Interests: Yearning, childbirth, suicide.

Oh, her! Yes, a handsome woman, wife of Karenin, the St Petersburg government official. I thought she threw herself under a ... Sshh!! Don't give away the ending.

But surely everyone knows that, fearing she has been supplanted in Vronsky's affections, she goes to the railway station ... No, they don't! In fact that book about her is currently top of the *New York Times, USA Today* and *Publisher's Weekly* bestseller lists.

What, Leo Tolstoy's 838-page magnum opus finished in 1877 and now appearing in a new English translation by Richard Pevearand Larissa Volokhonsky? That's the one.

And why would so many Americans suddenly buy such a good book? Does there have to be a reason?

Yes. Well, Oprah Winfrey's book club has just recommended it.

Is it really wise for people without the proper training to be tackling two-and-a-half inches of 19th-century Russian literature? Oprah thinks so. "I believe we can do this," she said.

That's sweet. Did she like the book? Oh, she hasn't actually read it yet.

Outrageous! Oh no, it's actually very exciting. You see, she will now be reading the book alongside her audience for the first time ever.

That is exciting. Yes it is.

She'd better complete it. Oh, she will. She vows to "finish every page".

I bet the publishers are pleased. "We are thrilled by the rapid response that Oprah's viewers and avid readers have had for Anna Karenina," was how Norman Lidofsky put it.

Not villainous, moustachioed Count Lidofsky who was seen flirting with beautiful but unworldly Ekaterina Shcherbatskaya in the summer house? No. President of paperback sales at Penguin Lidofsky.

Not to be confused with: How Clean Is Your Dacha?, Profit From Property with Anton Chekhov, Fyodor Dostoyevsky's How to Cook and Speeding Steam Trains: a Rough Guide.

16/06/2004

~ PRINCE PHILIP ~

What's the old roister-doister/bigoted parasite done now? It's more a question of what's been done to him. He's sporting a first-class black eye.

Good heavens – drunk again? No, you're thinking of the Queen Mum.

Well, what explanation has been given for this unseemly shiner? Has the Duke been duking it out with someone? Who on earth would want to thump Prince Philip in the face? Oh, I don't know – the Chinese ('slitty-eyed), the Indians (they bodge electrical jobs), the Scots (all drunks), the Australian aborigines (still chucking spears, apparently), Michael Cashman, the African continent ... I could go on.

All right, all right, I'm not saying he doesn't know how to wind up a population or two, but none of them had a pop at the old man. What really happened then? According to an aide to the Duke of Edinburgh: "He slipped in the bath and caught the side of his eye with his thumb."

He jabbed himself in the eye with his own thumb? You do begin to fear for the future of the monarchy, don't you? It could happen to anyone. The good news is that, according to the aide, Philip said it didn't hurt.

So he's numb from the neck up - that's not hugely reassuring. Although it does explain the Windsors' tendency to talk without moving their jaws. But it's not the first time he's had a black eye either. He turned up for church in December 2002 with two such contusions, and a cut nose. Rumours of a fall abounded.

And then? He had a growth removed from his nose and the swelling made his eyes look black.

I still say the Queen could be pretty handy with her fists. Don't be ridiculous. She'd use her handbag.

Not to be confused with: Black-eyed peas, black-eyed Susans, black-eyed Sallys, Ol' Blue Eyes, a panda.

27/10/2004

~ IDS ~

Age: 55.

Appearance: Overgrown baby,

William Hague's unidentical twin.

Name rings a bell. But I can't remember why. Former Tory leader?

There have been so many. Mad staring eyes?

You'll have to narrow it down a bit.

Bald one?

Keep going.

Never drank 14 pints in a day . . .

You're really not helping.

. . . and didn't come from Yorkshire.

That one! I thought he was running a golf course. He looks the sort.

No, a think tank. He was all over the place yesterday, plugging its new 370-page report.

Blimey, what was that about? The need to jail infant asylum seekers?

You really must stop thinking of the Conservatives as the nasty party. Duncan Smith's Centre for Social Justice is working towards 'a reversal of social breakdown in the UK'. Yes, the MP for Chingford and Woodford Green has been putting a fatherly arm around the nation and warning us about destructive lifestyles, the culture of dependency, families where three generations are without work, and so on. The thing is, he wants to help 'Britain's broken society', not punish it.

Britain's broken society? I thought that was David Cameron's line.

Well, yes and no. Cameron did bang on about it a couple of years ago, but he was less interested in benefits than booze and broken homes. IDS is calling for radical yet touchy-feely reform of the welfare system.

Margaret "there's no such thing as society" Thatcher must be turning in her grave . . . She's still alive, remember. In fact, she's sitting right behind you in a tank!

Ha, you almost had me going. The only tanks Tories like these days are ones they think in.

Do say: "Work is the sustainable route out of poverty. Unless we put the system right now, we run the risk of increasing the number of residually unemployed".

Don't say: "Are you the really boring one who loves cricket?"

17/09/2009

~ SIMON COWELL ~

Age: 50 next Wednesday.

Appearance: Stocky little 49-year-old fella with a mouthful of Persil-white teeth and a brain that can calculate the royalties over a singer's lifetime in the time it takes his victim to complete three bars of a power ballad while his black eyes close in a single, styptic blink.

I know the one you mean! Judge on The X Factor. Pop

Idol. American Idol. Britain's Got No Talent. Used to wear his trousers up around his armpits. Sssh. We never speak of the trousers. Simon doesn't like it.

Why do we care what he likes? Because he's richer than God and controls TV. If he takes against the human race, he will withdraw the teat from which we suckle. And without the mindless adoration of millions every Saturday night Cheryl Cole will wither, flutter to the ground and die. Die! Do you want that on your conscience?

To be honest, I'd survive. Fifty on Wednesday, eh? Is he having a party? But of course – organised, but not paid for (Simon's been very clear on that), by his new bezzie mate Sir Philip Green, the kajillionaire with whom he formed a multimedia entertainment company this summer. It's a 250-grand bash for 400 of his closest friends at Wrotham Park. Elton John, Denise Richards, Kate Moss, Kylie Minogue, Donald Trump and his ex Sinitta are all invited – but Simon says he doesn't want any presents.

Cor – I bet they'll get two colours of jelly and everything! Has anyone been pointedly snubbed? It's not a party if nobody's been pointedly snubbed. The first X Factor winner, Steve Brookstein, has been emphatically not invited. All Simon's other singing Frankenstein's monsters are coming, but he and Steve fell out years ago and Simon is not a man to forget or forgive. There are people who made trouser jibes back in 2001 who are still living under assumed names in Cuba.

Sounds like a great night. It will be. Three Rat Pack impersonators are being flown in from Las Vegas too.

Is there nothing money can't buy? No.

Do say: "Happy birthday! I know you said no presents but I saw these low-rise jeans and thought of you."

Don't say: "Hi Simon – it's Steve. Let me in – please?"

~ DAVID DIMBLEBY ~

Age: 71 at the end of the month.

Appearance: Character actor often called upon to play venerable broadcaster.

Profession: Venerable broadcaster.

I know – made broadcasts from Normandy during the D-Day landings, broke into television, hosted Panorama in the 50s. You're thinking of his Dad, Richard Dimbleby.

Oh. Is he the one who's always sucking up to Prince Charles?

No, that's his younger brother, Jonathan. So he's the one who does all those animal programmes?

Now you're confusing Dimblebys with Attenboroughs. I'm prone to that.

Which one is he? He's the BBC's longstanding safe pair of hands.

And what does that entail? Commentating on the state opening of parliament, the Trooping of the Colour, the last seven general elections, the funerals of Princess Diana and the Queen Mother, that sort of thing.

Any tricky assignments on the horizon? Yes, now you mention it. Dimbleby will be hosting Question Time this week.

Has he never done it before? He's done it for the last 15 years, but this week the panel will feature BNP leader Nick Griffin.

Racist! Save your interjections for Thursday, when Dimbleby faces the thankless task of not allowing Griffin a platform for his odious views, or an opportunity to retreat from his odious views, or the chance to come across as either a respectable politician or a victim of liberal bias.

It can't be done. That's why a lot of people, Welsh secretary Peter Hain to name one, think it's a mistake to allow Griffin on in the first place.

What does Dimbleby say? Nothing so far. He takes his impartiality seriously.

How seriously? "I never tell anyone how I vote," he says. "Not my children. Nor my wife."

Journalism runs in his blood, I suppose. Indeed. The family firm, the Dimbleby Newspaper Group, was sold in 2001 for a reported £8m.

Do say: "You're undoubtedly the best man to preside over this fiasco."

Don't say: "What are those meerkats like up close?"

20/10/2009

~ PAULA RADCLIFFE ~

Age: 35.

Appearance: Tear-stained.

What, again? She's always crying, that one.

When did the tears start? In the 2004 Olympics she cried when she was forced to drop out of the marathon four miles from the finish line. The second time was last year, after she barely made it to the end of the Bejing Olympics marathon. And the latest was on Sunday, when she finished fourth in the New York marathon, having been plagued with knee problems throughout.

You know, if she hates running so much, she should just give it up. Take it from me, there's far more pleasure in a packet of Tunnock's teacakes. She doesn't hate running.

Really? Even though it's got no chocolate, biscuity base or marshmallow centre at all? Why the tears then? Gosh, I don't know. Maybe she was ambushed in New York by a scary ghost left over from Halloween. Maybe she suddenly remembered in Athens the bit in the film where Bambi's mother dies. Or perhaps, when you are pushing yourself to mental and physical extremes during a race against the best of the best, when you're endeavouring to demonstrate to yourself, to your country and to the world that you can succeed in the activity to which you have dedicated more or less your entire life and things suddenly go totally tits up, an athlete will occasionally find him or herself a teensy bit overwhelmed.

It's usually women, though, isn't it? They just can't cope. Yes, of course. Apart from Gazza, when he was booked in the 1990 World Cup semi-final. And Roger Federer crying in defeat at the Australian Open and triumph at the French this year. Cristiano Ronaldo has been awash on more than one occasion. Across the pond, basketball players such as Glen Davis and Kobe Bryant have all been knee-deep in tears – and their knees are very high up. I could go on.

I stand corrected. Thank you. Have a teacake.

Do say: Better luck next time, Paula.

Don't say: Tendonitis-schmendonitis! You should just run through the pain.

~ KANYE WEST ~

Age: 32.

Appearance: A jackass.

As in Equus asinus, the odd-toed ungulate beloved of hobby farmers and Italian sausage-makers? A donkey? What happened to "If you can't think of anything nice to say . . ."? I was merely quoting Barack Obama, 44th president of the United States. The great orator wheeled out the J-word a couple of months ago, after the rapper disrupted the MTV video music awards. Feel free to imagine some inverted commas.

It's all flooding back. West thought his friend Beyoncé should have won some statuette and grabbed the mic off the woman who did. She was so upset she couldn't finish her thank-you speech. That's it. West's victim was the 19-year-old country singer Taylor Swift. Obama has all her LPs, or something.

Didn't Pink call West a complete and utter bounder? Her precise words were: "Kanye West is the biggest piece of shit on earth." Katy Perry said it was as if he had "stepped on a kitten". To be fair, West phoned Swift to apologise.

Shouldn't he have shot them all? He's not that kind of rapper. He comes from a respectable middle-class family and never bust a cap in anyone's ass.

He's still a bit of a bozo, isn't he? He does tend to throw hissy-fits when things don't go his way, and for some reason it's usually at an MTV ceremony. In 2006, he stormed the stage after losing the best-video prize to Justice vs Simian. "If I don't win," he helpfully explained, "the awards show loses credibility." On the other hand, West has spoken out against homophobia, and he made some friends after Hurricane Katrina when he claimed that "President Bush doesn't care about black people".

I'm warming to him. How long till the next outburst? Just hours, with luck. Both he and Beyoncé are up for prizes at tonight's MTV Europe music awards. Swift's nominated too, though not for the same awards.

Do say: "Don't worry, Taylor: his people told my people that he's going to stay in and wash his beard."

Don't say: "Oh, Christ, he's here after all. And he's brought Jarvis Cocker."

05/11/2009

~ HERMAN VON ROMPUY ~

Age: 62.

Appearance: Retired headmaster, freshly goosed.

Former Dutch porn star? Star of those much-loved 70s flicks Canal Knowledge and Confessions of a Windmill Cleaner? Known to his admirers as Rompuy-Pompuy? Sometimes I don't think you take this column seriously. We can't afford to lose any more ads from Clogs express.

Go on, then: educate me. He's a former Belgian economist.

You have 10 seconds to convince everyone else to carry on reading. He's also favourite to become the first president of the European council when EU leaders meet tomorrow.

What's the appeal? a) He's not Tony Blair; b) no one has nightmares about plucky little Belgium taking over Europe; c) he does an attractive impersonation of a man who doesn't want the top job but will, if necessary, shoulder the burden; and

d) he's not Tony Blair.

That's twice you've mentioned Blair. Yes, but the British candidate does get up a lot of noses. Angela Merkel apparently calls him "Mr Flash".

What's he doing right now? Pretending to sort out the Middle East? Van Rompuy, you fool. He's the Belgian prime minister.

No wonder I hadn't heard of him. Is he any good? His wife says so. He wasn't keen to be PM, but King Albert II talked him into it last December after scandals and financial chaos brought down the government and almost tore the country apart. "Belgium still needs him," says Mrs van R.

What does this national saviour believe in? Christian Democracy. Europe-wide taxation. Sound economics. Caravan holidays and writing haikus.

I love short poems in languages I don't understand. Can you read us one? "Een meeuw op één poot /starend staande in de zee. / De kou deert haar niet."

What did that mean? "Gravy train departs / As Tony fumes on platform. / I'm on board, ha ha."

Seriously? No. It might be about cats.

Do say: "If Belgium needs a PM, my mate Tony's at a bit of loose end."

Don't say: "I loved you in Two Hips From Amsterdam."

18/11/2009

~ THOUGHT FOR THE DAY ~

Age: 39.

Appearance: Triumphant, but trying to hide it.

Let's just cut to the chase today. What's occurring? Well, good morning John, and good morning Evan, and good morning everybody. A funny thing happened to me on the way to the synagogue yesterday . . .

What *are* you on about? Would you like me to fetch your medication? That was my witty and instantly recognisable homage to Rabbi Lionel Blue. To answer your next few questions, he's the best-known contributor to Thought for the Day, a three-minute slot in the middle of the Today programme; yes, that tedious bit when religious types link current events to their holy texts; no, you're not the only one who goes to the toilet to avoid it; and yes, that preaching does stick out like a sore thumb on Radio 4.

If you don't pace yourself there'll be an awful lot of white space at the bottom of this column. Why is it in the news? The BBC Trust has just turned down calls to open it to non-believers. The National Secular Society had complained the corporation was breaching its duty of impartiality.

What does that self-proclaimed "angry agnostic" John Humphrys say about the decision? I'll have to press you. He'd quite like Radio 4 to set up a separate slot for humanists, atheists and other such hell-bound types. "The obvious problem with that," however, "is that the whole nature of the beast changes and then it becomes just another signed essay."

When that man sits on a fence, it knows it's been sat

on. And the National Secular Society? It's threatening legal action: 'This is so blatant an abuse of religious privilege that we cannot simply let it pass.'

Isn't anyone pleased? The Almighty's absolutely delighted, though you'll have to take my word for it.

Do say: 'Verily, it is easier for a camel to go through the eye of a needle than for a sceptic to enter the 7.45am God-slot.'

Don't say: "If we can just bring back stoning we'll really have the unbelievers on the run."

19/11/2009

~ LADY GAGA ~

Age: 23.

Appearance: Topshop sales assistant trying to convince a credulous police officer she's an extraterrestrial being.

It's a great look, and one adopted behind closed doors by a surprising variety of people – so why should I care about her? Because she's been awarded the highest honour available to a pop singer.

The Victoria Cross? No, you dolt, a slot at the Royal Variety Performance.

Her Maj is a big fan, then? There has been no public statement from Buckingham Palace, though we suggest Prince Philip take some beta-blockers before the show. Goodness only knows what she will do for his blood pressure.

Foreign is she? Italian-American, but it's her racy stage act we're worried about. The Daily Telegraph reported that at the

MTV video awards she pretended to stab herself to death. Fake blood sprayed everywhere, and she ended up hanging from the ceiling. She's outrageous, you know.

I can't see how that would worry Prince Philip. Sounds suspiciously like the aftermath of a trip to the grouse moor, with her as the grouse. All right then, if you still don't believe she's a threat to the very fabric of society, you should read the *Daily Mail*. It reported that she's become a bad influence on Beyoncé.

How? By convincing her to record fewer great pop songs and more tedious ballads? No, by getting her to wear an eye mask and a Perspex bra in a video. Lady Gaga likes her peculiar costumes.

Oh, for goodness sake. Is that the best you can do? Listen, google Lady+Gaga+Outrage and you get 190,000 hits. Google Prince+Philip+Outrage and you only get 40,900 hits. Given the number of outrages he's been involved in, I'd say that's pretty clear evidence of her outrageousness.

Do say: "I used to buy my lingerie from La Perla, but I find Perspex so much more comfortable."

Don't say: "I'm sure Prince Harry will lend you one of his costumes for the show."

23/11/2009

~ CHRISTMAS TREES ~

Age: Approximately 500 years.

Appearance: Highly contested.

Contested? Highly. Deciding how to decorate the Christmas tree is the definitive household conflict. It's the culmination of a year of arguments; the decisive battle; the domestic equivalent of the D-day landings.

How so? Just like in the second world war, there are four schools of thought: Aryanism, British Imperialism, American Interventionism and Being Japanese.

Are those still related to Christmas trees? They're barely related to the second world war, but hear me out. First, the Arbroreal Aryans. Trees must be tall, colour-coordinated and symmetrical. They often spend several hours moving a single bauble back and forth between two branches less than an inch apart, before asking "What do you think?" and settling on the opposite.

Doesn't sound like me. What about the other three? The British Imperialist tree is a patchwork of stolen colonial treasures combining to create a whole that makes about as much sense as a pink wafer canoe. They obey two simple rules: decorations must be as old and mismatched as possible, and so numerous that the branches point vertically down under their weight. They won't stop until it looks like a giant green squid making off with the entire contents of a jumble sale.

Being Japanese? The minimalist approach. They favour a bare tree, with nothing but a single string of white lights that may twinkle, but not flash.

I don't qualify for any of these. Then you must be an American Interventionist, someone who confuses Christmas with Miniature Las Vegas Month. I'm guessing your tree's in your front garden covered in garish lights?

They're not garish – they're festive. Is there, by any chance, a reindeer made of lightbulbs on your roof?

All nine of them, baby! Everybody hates you.

Do say: "That second world war analogy wasn't needlessly confusing at all."

Don't say: "When is Miniature Las Vegas Month?"

07/12/2009

~ THE EURO ~

Age: 8.

Appearance: Foreign.

That funny money they use on the other side of the Channel? The one that replaced French francs and the like in 2002? That's the stuff. It's legal tender in 16 European countries, as well as pretend states such as Monaco and Vatican City. But have you heard the news?

Is the government about to betray thousands of years of independence? Is the Queen furious at plans to abandon sterling? I couldn't get the *Sun* this morning. Much, much worse! The dream of a united Europe is turning into a nightmare! Things fall apart! The centre cannot hold! Mere anarchy is loosed upon the world!

I know Yeats is out of copyright, but could you put it more prosaically? There's a gap of several percentage points between German and Greek government bond yields!

Less prosaically? And without the exclamation marks? The euro's in trouble, and some of our neighbours are going to lose a lot of money. Their currency has fallen 10% against the dollar since November, thanks to speculators and economic turmoil in Portugal, Italy, Greece and Spain. The four countries are now known as the Pigs.

Because they're in sh-. Stop! Because of their initials. Since no one likes lending to someone who actually needs the money, the Pigs have to pay far more to borrow euros than France and Germany. The better-off countries may have to bail them out, and Greece may even need to turn to the International Monetary Fund. That would be almost as humiliating as that regrettable marbles business.

Are there any alternatives? Joseph Stiglitz, the economist who is advising the Greeks, wants governments to intervene in the markets to "teach the speculators a lesson".

Just like Britain did in the 1992 sterling crisis? You're not the first person to point out the similarities.

Remind me how that worked out. We lost £3.4bn. George Soros made more than $1bn.

Do say: "You know, Gordon Brown was right not to take Britain into the euro."

Don't say: "Mind you, even a stopped clock's correct every now and again."

09/02/2010

~ THE LADY ~

Age: Is that a question you'd ask a lady? I'll whisper it . . . 125 this year.

Speak up, I'm 93 and a little deaf. Exactly the sort of reader *The Lady* no longer wants, I'm afraid.

Don't be so insulting, young man. I've been reading the Lady since I was knee-high to an Irish wolfhound. My mother read it, too. Used it to recruit my nanny, governess, all our domestic staff. I remember Mr McCrindle, the butler, saying . . . Madam, we haven't got time for this. *The Lady* is now a whizzy, happening publication edited by Rachel Johnson, printed in full colour, and seeking to double its circulation by connecting the venerable magazine to the modern world.

I enjoyed it as it was. Ms Johnson, sister of Boris but less retiring than him, likened it to "a 1950s care home in Sark".

I've always adored Sark. Can we keep to the point please? "It looks like a Bupa catalogue," said Ms Johnson when she took over. "We must get away from using generic cover pictures of women with neat grey bobs. I'm going to put real women on the front, like Michelle Obama."

Is she one of the Somersetshire Obamas, Lady Doris's girls? Not as far as I know.

It sounds horrible. Johnson has admitted an article on the dos and don'ts of bedding your nanny may have been a mistake . . . Are you all right? Your face has gone purple.

Just a turn. Please hand me that nosegay. And what are they planning now? A special birthday issue honouring 125 "Ladies of Today".

People like Enid Trumpington-Smythe, who has run the Rutlandshire Bloodhounds since 1947? I don't think she made the cut. But lingerie mogul Jacqueline Gold, Carry On star Barbara Windsor and Strictly Come Dancing legend Arlene Phillips are all on the list . . . Lady Aspic, you look a very odd colour indeed. LADY ASPIC!! McCrindle, for God's sake, call an ambulance.

15/02/2010

~ THE READER'S DIGEST ~

Age: 72.

Appearance: Endangered.

I'm worried about that apostrophe. Shouldn't it be after the "s"? Even the Independent has at least two readers. Now you mention it, the Digest's circulation is more than a million less than it used to be. But it's still 465,000.

Crikey! I had no idea there were so many dentists' waiting rooms. So it's not in trouble, then? *Au contraire.* Its publisher has gone into administration, after failing to convince regulators it can patch a £125m hole in its pension fund.

What does that mean in plain English? It's not exactly bust, but bustedness is on the cards.

But I couldn't get through life without Reasons to be cheerful, Laughter is the best medicine and . . . And?

You know, it's years since I had my teeth looked at. What else will you find in Reader's Digest nowadays? The January issue had an "exclusive" interview with Kenneth Branagh, six "brilliant" new ways to lose weight, nine health niggles you can't ignore, five reasons why sex is good for you . .

. and 101 signs that God hates gays, by Jan Moir.

Really? No, I made that last one up. The magazine may resemble the *Daily Mail,* as one insider admits, but "without the nasty bits". It's even done its bit for public health: in the 1950s it helped to publicise the link between smoking and lung cancer.

Perhaps it does deserve to survive after all. How many jobs are at stake? 117 in London and Swindon, as well as 1,600 pensions.

And abroad? That's it. The American parent has been in trouble, but the only thing preventing its recovery was its exposure to its British arm. That's now, in effect, at an end.

So what will happen to the prize draw? How will the Royal Mail survive without all that rubbish to deliver? If you won the last draw, you'll get your reward. The administrators haven't decided whether any more will be held.

Do say: "This envelope could change your life!"

Don't say: "Please find enclosed your P45."

21/02/2010

~ SNOOP DOG ~

Age: 38.

Appearance: Anywhere he likes now.

Eh? An immigration tribunal has just overturned a three-year ban against the gangsta rapper entering the UK.

But he looks like exactly the kind of lovable eccentric Britain is crying out for. And his jewellery could cut the national debt by half. Why is he banned? Is it because he is, you know, ah . . . "urban"? No, It's because last time he came here, in 2006, he and five of his entourage were arrested at Heathrow for violent disorder.

Well, who hasn't got a little rambunctious when faced with the horrors of air travel? They smashed up the duty free area and injured eight police officers when they were told those with economy tickets could not go into the first-class lounge. Snoop was cautioned, although he was also seen on film taken at the time entertaining children at the airport.

Fo' shizzle my nizzle! Don't. Just don't.

Sorry. Still – a total ban seems harsh. If we stopped every celebrity who threw a strop during an international flight we would have no Gillian Anderson, no Amy Winehouse, Peter Buck, Diana Ross or Naomi Campbell. We'd be a cultural desert! Well, thanks to Snoop's legal team, who successfully argued that the ban affected their client's right to freedom of expression under Article 10 of the Human Rights Act, we look set to remain a lushly green and fertile land.

Hurrah! And what will he be freely expressing, d'you think? His further thoughts on Hoes, Money and Clout or Payin' for Pussy, perhaps, if tracks from his 1998 album are anything to go by. Or on Break[ing] a Bitch Til I Die (2001's Duces'n Trayz)?

Hmm. This human rights thing is a little tricky sometimes, isn't it? It is. But Snoop still needs a visa. And his previous multiple convictions for drug and gun offences may mean he is refused.

I didn't know about those. And although he was cleared, the murder trial in 1993 probably won't help either.

Gulp. Can I shizzle my nizzle now, please? Yes. Yes, you may.

Do say: "Snoop, how lovely to see you – it's been too long!"

Don't say: "Snoop! You haven't come here to kill me, have you?"

09/03/2010

~ THE DEWEY SYSTEM ~

Zzzzzzzzzzzzzzz: Wake up, this is going to be more interesting than you think.

OK, sorry, I was still in bank holiday mode. Age? 134.

Appearance: Orderly.

Something to do with libraries, isn't it? Spot on. It's the world's most used method of cataloguing books.

I thought you said this was going to be interesting. It is. This is a seminal moment for librarianship. For 134 years, geeky men with acne and prematurely aged women in spectacles have quietly gone about cataloguing books according to the principles of Melvil Dewey, largely ignored by the rest of us. But now rock legend Keith Richards has admitted to a passion for librarianship, and a failed attempt to apply the Dewey system to his own large private library.

Keith Richards of the Rolling Stones? The very same. In his autobiography, he reveals that books were his first love, and calls public libraries "a great equaliser".

Sympathy for the librarian? Indeed.

Little Red Rooster? Shhhhhhhhhh.

Wild Horses? Try 798, under equestrianism.

798? The Dewey system breaks human knowledge down into 10 broad categories, such as philosophy, religion, science and literature, then subdivides each into further batches of 10, more or less ad infinitum. Take music: that comes under arts and recreation (700) and is assigned the number 780. You'll find rock music at 781.66, and the Rolling Stones and Keith Richards will form subsets of that.

Who was Melvil Dewey? A crazy American autodidact who invented the system in his 20s and is known as the "father of librarianship".

Melvil? His real name was Melville, but another of his pet projects was the simplification of the English language. He wanted to eliminate all superflus letrs.

Do say: "No problem, sir, you'll find it at 432.89718329."

Don't say: "No idea, I think it's on the top shelf in Miscellaneous, somewhere between Penguins of Patagonia and Advanced Bidding Strategies in Contract Bridge."

~ DON QUIXOTE ~

Name: Donkey Shotty.

Pardon? No? Didn't I get it right? Don Heeoaty? Is that how you say it?

Oh, you mean Don Quixote? Yes! I meant Don Qui … wait, are you supposed to pronounce the "x" or not?

Age: Listen, I'm clearly not good with words. How do you expect me to cope with numbers?

It's "Don Quixote", by the way. Say it with me. Don … Dowww– oh, it's no good. I can't pronounce his bloody name. In fact, you know what? Nobody can.

Related: Can you pronounce the names of these literary characters?

He's the eponymous character of one of history's most famous books. Everyone can pronounce it. Well, I can't, and nor can loads of other people.

Really? According to a survey by Audible, yes. Almost half the 2,000 people quizzed had trouble getting his name right.

That's unusual. No, it isn't. Literature is littered with all sorts of confusing names that readers can't understand until they have been said aloud. Before the the Game of Thrones TV series came along, for example, nobody alive knew how to pronounce Daenerys Targaryen.

Interesting. Any other examples? Hermione from Harry Potter was in the top 10.

Seriously? People actually called her Hermy-won? Look, stop being so high and mighty. Names can be difficult sometimes.

But Hermione is an actual name that actual people have. It's not like she's got a made-up name like Voldemort or anything. I think you mean "Voldemorr".

What? That's how JK Rowling says it's meant to pronounced. With a silent "t", like Stephen Colbert.

A silent "t"? That sounds like bullshi. You see how easily it's done, though? The way you interpret a written word is highly subjective. Mistakes are made all the time.

Fine, I take your point. It's pronounced Don Key-Hoh-Tey, by the way. Thank you. Now, what have we learned from all this?

We've learned that it's unrealistic to expect people to be able to pronounce names that they've never heard before. Some might even call it quixotic. You mean key-hoh-tic?

No, quixotic, with an "x". It's a real word. Look it up, idiot. Oh, for goodness sake.

Do say: "Don Quixote."

Don't say: "Don Quixote."

12/10/2015

~ THOMAS PAINE ~

Age: 72. Or 278, had he lived.

Appearance: Very ... rights-y.

Thomas Paine! Founding father of a little place I like to call the United States of America! That's the one.

"Corset-maker by trade, a journalist by profession and a propagandist by inclination," I believe he has been called. Indeed. And born in Thetford, Norfolk, would you believe?

Well, that I did not know! Is this news to all? Is that why we're talking about him? No. He's in the news because he has been accused of plagiarism.

What monstrous calumny is this? Who besmirches the name of the man who virtually won the American revolution for George Washington? A historian at the University of Kansas, called Jonathan Clark.

What does this scoundrel claim? That the 6,000 words about the French revolution in Paine's famous 1791 publication, Rights of Man, were written by the Marquis de Lafayette.

Of Lafayette, Texas? No.

Louisiana? No.

Indiana? California? No – it's the title of French aristocrat Gilbert du Motier, a close friend of Washington, Hamilton and Jefferson and a military officer who fought for the US in the revolutionary war. He is known to have provided material for other parts of The Rights of Man.

So *quoi*? That doesn't mean he wrote a great big,

super-famous chunk of it. *Non, mais* Clark does point out that its unusually "eloquent, idealistic and visionary" tone stands out from the rest of the book.

Maybe Paine had had a soupcon of sherry by that point. He worked very hard, you know. In that section, "Paine" also boasts of knowing the "secret history" of French politics, which, as a low-born man unable to speak French at that time, he would not have done.

Well, *peut-être* ... And "it reads like the English prose of a native-born French speaker".

Oh, nonsense! What next? Shakespeare didn't write Shakespeare? Katie Price didn't write Being Jordan? Leonardo da Vinci didn't paint The Da Vinci Code? Sit down for a moment, could you? We have much to discuss.

Do say: "The Gettysburg address. That's still stirring, unsullied stuff."

Don't say: "These are the times that try men's souls, eh, Tom? Hey, why are you writing that down?"

18/09/2015

~ THE TIMESHARE ~

Age: In its mid-50s.

Appearance: Dead on its feet.

What? The timeshare is dead? But I'm part of a lovely little scheme. You're one of a dying breed, then. Brits are cancelling their timeshare plans in droves, at a rate of six a day.

But why? The world is a huge expanse of unexplored crevices, my friend. It's yours for the taking. Why anyone would prefer to return to the exact same villa in the exact same week of every year is beyond me.

But it's a nice villa, near a shop. The beach is 10 minutes away, and we know where all the plug sockets are. Get with the programme. Even the chief executive of the Timeshare Association says the current system is "in the doldrums".

But we agreed to it years ago, and I think it's contractually binding for ever, so even my great-grandchildren will have to go to this villa until they die. You might want to get that looked at, actually. Last year, the EU ruled that about 12% of all timeshare schemes were illegal, which means you might be due a refund.

We're free! We're finally free! Congratulations. You are now one of the thousands of holidaymakers finally unshackled from the tyranny of the timeshare.

Ooh, where should we go next then? Well, ahem, have you heard about the points-based timeshare?

No, but do tell. A bunch of timeshare resorts have pooled together, and your investment buys points that you can exchange for stays in any of them.

Wouldn't it be easier to just book a different holiday each year? No, you see, you don't get any points on a regular holiday, do you? You know what everyone loves?

Points? Points! One year, you could go skiing, the next year, you could have a cruise. The whole world is open to you, and all it takes is a multi-year financial commitment on your part.

This still sounds a bit restrictive. It's not! It's just points. Points are great, right? Points never did any harm to anyone.

Great! Where do I sign? Just let me dip this quill into virgin blood …

Do say: "The timeshare is dead."

Don't say: "Long live the timeshare."

10/02/2016

~ OFFICE TEMPERATURES ~

Age: It's been going on, quietly, for decades.

Appearance: Legions of shivering victims, huddled in corners with shawls on.

Who is this war between? Men and women. In offices.

Ah. And what's it about? The pay gap? Sexual harassment? Statutory maternity leave? The glass ceiling? The air conditioning.

The air conditioning? The women are cold. The men not so much.

So it's not a real war. The problem is real enough, according to a study published in Nature Climate Change: women are suited to an average office temperature about 3C warmer than men.

Someone did a study of that? Yes. Professor Boris Kingma of Maastricht University studied 16 women performing "light office work".

Sounds as if the professor needs to keep his eyes on his computer, before someone complains to HR. He was studying them in a climate chamber. For science.

What were his findings? He found that women had a significantly lower metabolic rate than men. Men are comfortable – neither sweating nor shivering – at about 22C. Women, on the other hand, find that a bit chilly.

What's the problem? Turn the dial down a notch. The problem is that climate control in office buildings is based on a comfort standard first set in the 1960s, which was in turn based on the metabolic rate of a 40-year old, 70kg man.

That's so sexist. Sexist, and wasteful. Offices have been kept cooler than they need to be for years because we've failed to take into account the actual metabolic values of a huge chunk of the workforce.

Are there any other advantages to making the men sweat a little? Yes. Another study from 2004 found that people working in warmer conditions – 25C, as opposed to 22C – make fewer typing mistakes and have increased productivity.

25C it is, then. Fine, as long as you're aware that means more men wearing shorts in the office during summer.

Hmm. On balance, I think it might be better to put a box of free pashminas near the lifts. Put it in an email, and we can raise it at the next meeting.

Do say: "Let's work together to reduce gender-discriminating bias in thermal comfort predictions."

Don't say: "Sorry about all the mistakes. It's hard to type with these mittens on."

04/08/2015

~ SALLY THE CASH MACHINE ~

Age: Already too old for this joke of a world.

Appearance: Hard to say, since your vision will involuntarily blur and darken upon sight of her.

That bad? It sounds as if you're just talking about a cash machine. You don't understand. It's a cash machine called Sally (or sometimes Mike or Jake). The things have names.

Why does it have a name? It's part of a new Barclays initiative in a handful of branches to get customers used to its assisted service counters, which are basically gussied-up ATMs.

And why don't they just call the machines assisted service counters? Because that makes them sound chilling and totalitarian, like their onscreen options would include "Receive lethal injection" and "Obey your faceless masters".

So, what exactly is the problem with calling them "Sally"? Because it's so twee. It doesn't credit customers with any intelligence. It's less a cash machine and more a cross between an Innocent smoothie bottle and the Terminator.

What's wrong with Innocent smoothie bottles? Have you read the back of one? It's like someone has dictated the ambient thoughts of the world's most insufferable three-year-old.

Are we getting off-subject here? No, it's all part of the same problem. These gigantic, terrifying corporations are trying to endear themselves to us by making themselves as infuriatingly cutesy and infantile as possible. It started with smoothies; now, it's bank machines. Next thing you know, GlaxoSmithKline will be renaming itself Mr Glitterchop's Yummy-Wummy Medicine Company.

I think you might be overreacting. I'm not. Barclays is getting rid of flesh-and-blood bank workers and giving folksy names to their robot replacements in the hope that we won't be able to tell the difference.

If you hate it so much, why don't you stop banking with Barclays? Oh, because it's too complicated. All my Etsy money is paid into a Barclays account.

You have an Etsy page? Yes. I make artisan, heart-shaped bunting that spells out the phrase: "I Wuv Ooh, Snuggle-Bear."

Really? Look, it's different. It is.

Do say: "This is a cash machine. Its name is 'Cash Machine'."

Don't say: "Press one to display your balance, two for a withdrawal or three for a big cuddle."

~ DONALD TRUMP ~

Age: Man – 69. Hair – tests inconclusive on material unknown to science.

Appearance: 69-year-old man wearing dead alien animal on his head.

Has he died? Only from the hairline up. The rest of him is too rich to die.

What has he done then? Announced that he is running for US president.

Doesn't he do this every year? Regardless of whether or not there's a presidential race? Yes, but this time it's official. On a stage in the basement of Trump Tower in Manhattan, surrounded by eight American flags, to the soundtrack of Neil Young's Rockin' in the Free World, Donald Trump told the world that he is running for president. And Young told the world that Trump did not have permission to use his music.

OK, so what's Trump promising? To get rid of Obamacare.

That's a given. What else? To take back America, which Obama has reduced to the level of a third-world country and handed over to the Chinese, whose leaders hopelessly outclass Uncle Sam's. It's like "the New England Patriots and Tom Brady [versus] a high-school team," says Donald.

Ah, Trump truth. Splendid. And he's going to stop Mexico "sending us all the wrong people".

Let me guess. Does it involve a wall? Yes! Are you psychic? It involves "a great, great wall on our southern border, and I will make Mexico pay for that wall".

Anything else? He's going to cut spending on education,

massively. "People are tired of spending more money on education per capita than any other country."

Yes, that is a national disgrace. And he's going to be "the greatest jobs president that God ever made" and reduce the real goddamn unemployment rate from 20%.

I thought the US unemployment rate was 5.4%? That's just the official government figure. Trump believes it to be 18-20%, so that is what he is going to reduce it from.

I see. Anything else before I go and drive myself off a cliff? He has disclosed, in accordance with legislation, that he is worth $8.73bn and will be using his own money to try to buy the presidency.

You mean, run his campaign? Tomato, tomahto.

Do say: "Stephen Colbert – your country needs you."

Don't say: "No it doesn't – satire is dead."

17/06/2015

~ RECEP TAYYIP ERDOGAN ~

Age: 61.

Appearance: For legal reasons, it's best to describe his appearance as "Someone who definitely doesn't own any golden toilets".

That's it? This is the worst game of Guess Who ever. This is about Recep Tayyip Erdogan, president of Turkey.

Right. And he's famous for not owning any golden toilets? Yes. Recep Tayyip Erdogan definitely does not own any golden toilets. I really can't make that clear enough.

That's funny, because he looks like the type of man who would probably own at least one golden toilet. Don't say that! You never accuse Recep Tayyip Erdogan of owning a golden toilet. Never!

Why not? Because he'll sue you. At a rally on Saturday, opposition leader Kemal Kiliçdaro lu implied that Erdogan went to the toilet on a gold-plated seat, and now Erdogan is demanding the equivalent of £24,000 in compensation from him.

So that he can buy himself a golden toilet? Is that how much they cost? No! Stop saying that! Any more of this and we'll be in deep trouble.

Why? We can stump up £24,000, can't we? We could do a Kickstarter. It's worse than that. We're also a newspaper. And if there's one thing that Recep Tayyip Erdogan hates more than people who accuse him of owning a golden toilet, it's newspapers.

How so? A Turkish newspaper recently published a video apparently showing Turkey's state intelligence helping to arm Syrian rebels, an act it had previously denied. And now Erdogan wants the editor jailed for life for "crimes against the government".

Yeesh. Is there anything about him that we can say? Well, he's on record as saying that women and men should not be treated equally because "it goes against the laws of nature" and that Israel is worse than Hitler, so there's that.

I'm starting to think that Recep Tayyip Erdogan might not be such a great guy. Don't say that. He's ace! He once threatened to destroy Twitter in a show of nationalistic might, for instance.

Well, fair's fair, I guess. Give him all the golden toilets

he needs. Stop it!

Do say: "Recep Tayyip Erdogan does not own any golden toilets."

Don't say: "But he wipes his bum on a mink rug. Can we say that? No?"

04/06/2015

~ GOD ~

Age: Ageless.

Appearance: Well, now you're asking. Rare, certainly. Last embodied, sort of, more than 2,000 years ago. Allegedly.

Why's He in the news? Don't tell me He's averted some kind of humanitarian crisis at freaking last? Come to the aid of the poor and needy? Smitten a few of those who are long overdue being smited? Got His arse into gear at last in any way? I'm afraid I have to take issue with your phraseology there.

Don't tell me – at the secular, liberal, all-must-have-prizes, drooping, dripping bloody Guardian you don't capitalise the 'h' in 'He'. I should have known. I wish I could smite every last one of you personally. Then you're going to love this. It shouldn't even be 'he' at all.

With all due sense of impending fury, contempt and dread I ask – what should it be? She.

You are the living end. It's not us, though. People in the Church of England are saying it.

Which people? Bring them before me. The pressure group Watch – Women and the Church – are arguing that it is more inclusive to refer to God as "she". Calling him – or her, or it, or whatever – "he" all the time suggests that men are closer to God.

Have you *seen* how many parliamentary and FTSE 100 positions we have? We ARE closer to God. That's obviously the way He wants it. The conception of God as a man raises a lot of complex issues – linguistically, theologically, about patriarchal power structures, of historical prejudice. Changing the language of worship is a step towards recognising if not solving some of them.

God's a man. Big beard, white robe, on a cloud. Problem solved. That's not a terrifically useful approach to broadening our understanding of the divine.

That's good, because I'm not interested in broadening our understanding of the divine. I understand Him just fine. Do you not think that's a little egocentric? If you believe in God, is the idea not that he/she/it is more than you can ever understand? Is that not the basic premise of most faiths?

Not mine. Bloody Anglicans. They're the Guardian newspaper of Christianity. D'you think the Catholics are recruiting. Always. Mind how you go.

Do say: "God surely transcends mere binary gender divisions."

Don't say: "Well, are we going to capitalise 'she'?"

01/06/2015

~ THE ERASER ~

Name: The eraser.

Age:

Appearance: Damning.

Eraser? Are you pretending to be American? It's a rubber. A rubber. But some people think that's a condom.

Only Americans. Enough with the cultural cringe. Assert yourself. OK, well, whatever – erasers, rubbers, or india rubbers, to give them their original name.

That's slightly imperialist. There's no pleasing you, is there? Whatever you call them, Guy Claxton wants them banned.

Who's Guy Claxton? A cognitive scientist and visiting professor at King's College London.

Why does he want them banned? Is it a health and safety issue? Are children gazing at them in bafflement and trying to use them as iPad props? Was he attacked by one as a child? He says the eraser "is an instrument of the devil because it perpetuates a culture of shame about error. It's a way of lying to the world, which says, 'I didn't make a mistake. I got it right first time.'"

It erases the truth! And the opportunity and ability to reflect on and learn from the learning process itself! Exactly. According to Claxton, erasers should be banned and mistakes acknowledged as part of a wider move towards schools preparing students for real life and not just exams.

They do say failure is the best teacher. I always thought that was because they had met my teachers. They were a motley crew. No, it's because setbacks and errors throw you back on your own resources and build character, which you need as you grow up and no one is there to shepherd you from multiple-choice question to multiple-choice question or from retake to retake.

I was prepared to mock the man who wanted to ban basic stationery items. But I acknowledge my mistake. Now that my ignorance of his motivation has been erased, I see him for what he truly is. Something between a valuable repository of sound common sense and a pedagogical visionary?

Precisely so, yes. Marvellous. What an unexpectedly positive note to end on! Let's have more of these!

Do say: "You don't need rubbers to bounce back from your mistakes!"

Don't say: "Failure is not an option. Especially if by 'rubbers' you mean 'condoms'."

27/05/2015

~ ART GARFUNKEL ~

Name: Art Garfunkel.

Age: 73.

Appearance: Dandelion seed head, after three good blows.

Occupation: Singer, bitter old man.

Bitter about what? Paul Simon, mostly.

Still? After all these years? It would seem so. In a recent interview with the Daily Telegraph he said that, by being nice to Paul Simon, he had "created a monster".

A hugely gifted, critically acclaimed, universally well-regarded, 12-Grammy-winning monster. That's the guy.

Is that really what Garfunkel meant to say? I know how these things can be taken out of context and twisted. He claimed he felt sorry for Simon because he was short, and befriended him as a compensation. "And that compensation gesture created a monster. End of interview."

Not much room for a generous interpretation of that. No. Of Simon's ongoing reluctance to reunite professionally, he said: "How can you walk away from this lucky place on top of the world, Paul? What's going on with you, you idiot? How could you let that go, jerk?"

He and Simon go back a long way, don't they? They had their first hit together, as Tom and Jerry, in 1957, and went on to score a string a mega-hits before splitting up in 1970.

I guess if I owed my whole career to someone else's immense song-writing talent, I would be bitter too. The thing is, Garfunkel has plenty of other strings to his bow. He has had solo hits, and he's given creditable acting performances in films including Carnal Knowledge and Bad Timing.

Versatile. Yup. At the height of his fame in the 1970s, he even did a stint as a maths teacher.

And he does have that angelic singing voice. He did until he was afflicted with a paresis of the vocal cords in 2010 that left him unable to sing a note.

How terrible. But he is largely back to his old self these days, and is touring the UK in September.

Sounds as if things are looking up. What's he got to be so grumpy about?

It seems that is just what he's like. At the height of his vocal troubles he said: "If I can't sing, I'm just an asshole."

Do say: "Whoo-hoo! We love you, Art! Do Bright Eyes!

Don't say: "Now you're an asshole who can sing."

25/05/2015

~ WALES ~

Name: Wales

Age: As a national identity, about 1,600 years old; as a devolved political entity, 16.

Appearance: Land mass to the left of England, approximately the size of Wales.

Never been. What's it like? Neurotic.

That's odd – I was sure you were going to say "rainy". The weather may be rainy, but the people are neurotic.

What do you mean by neurotic, exactly? You know – moody, depressed, temperamental.

I feel like that a lot of the time. You should move to Wales. You'll fit right in.

How can you possibly confer a single personality trait on a whole nation? They're not just neurotic. They're also extroverted and unconscientious.

Where are you getting your information from? The Big Personality Test.

And how big was this personality test? It was the largest ever study of the psychological landscape of the UK: 400,000 people took part, across 380 local authorities.

How did they find these people? They selected themselves by filling out an online questionnaire designed to measure their personalities against five established traits.

I see. This is nonsense, isn't it? Not at all. The study was carried out by Cambridge scientists and their findings were published in the journal Plos One.

But I should be taking the results with a pinch of salt, right? No need. They prove once and for all that the Welsh are neurotic, the Scots agreeable and Londoners lazy and unwelcoming.

What about the folks of Northern Ireland? Generally averse to surveys – they didn't provide enough data for researchers to draw any conclusions.

Is there any point in attempting to discover if people from one place share a regional character? Psychological traits can have health implications. "Conscientious people are more risk-averse, and more likely to get medical help early on when they have symptoms," said lead researcher Jason Rentfrew. "On the other hand, less conscientious people are more like to blow things off."

Those Welsh, always blowing things off. That's not just a Welsh trait – it's also popular in Manchester.

Wow. It's like lazy stereotyping, only much more specific. It's called science, mate.

Do say: "Welcome to Wales, land of rain and anxiousness."

Don't say: "Cheer up Cardiff! It might never happen!"

2505/2015

~ GARY ~

Age: Most likely in his 50s or 60s.

Appearance: Rarer and rarer.

Sorry, which Gary are we talking about? All the Garys. Everyone called Gary. The Human Garynome, if you will.

I won't. But I get the picture. What's happening to them? Is there a new deadly virus that only attacks Garys? Thankfully, no. But at the end of the day, the Gary is only human, and not enough new Garys are being created to replace the ones who die.

Why not? Parents just don't like the name any more. Gary reached its peak in the US in the early 1950s, when it was at one time the 12th most popular boy's name, with more than 38,000 appearing every year. There were even 90 girls named Gary in 1947.

Many of them no doubt in homage to Gary Cooper. Ah yes, one of the all-time great Garys, (though he was actually born a Frank). In England and Wales, the peak came later, in 1964, when Gary was 16th on the list.

And what's the situation now? Desperate. Gary has plummeted from view on both sides of the Atlantic, and is now severely endangered. Just 450 were created in the US in 2013, and 28 in England and Wales. Numbers will be swollen slightly by some of the more relaxed Gareths and Garths, but they too are endangered species. On current trends there may be no new Garys within a decade or two, and none left alive by the beginning of the 22nd century.

Habitat loss. Is that what we're talking about? In a way. There are still some very well-known Garys of course, such as

Lineker, Oldman, Barlow and Kemp.

Although that is basically a list of men who had their heyday in the 1980s and 1990s. Exactly. Overexposure around that time has harmed many great names. In 2013, English and Welsh parents created just 17 Roys, 15 Keiths, seven Kevins and three Traceys.

Three! I'm afraid so. Compare that with 110 Jaxsons, 167 Romeos, 2,211 Siennas, 3,264 Leos and 4,511 Oscars.

So we've basically become nations of losers. I blame the cocktail umbrella! I thought you might.

Do say: "Is it time to establish a small breeding population of Garys in London zoo?"

Don't say: "That would be cruel. Garys must be left free to roam in the wild."

10/05/2015

~ COLD CALLING ~

Age: As old as telephones.

Appearance: Frequent, unsolicited, ill-timed and full of promise.

What kind of promise? Freshly double-glazed windows, unique investment opportunities, consolidated debt.

No, thank you. What about some compensation for your recent personal injury?

I haven't had a recent personal injury. Just press 5 to speak to the refund team, who will process your refund today.

I'm hanging up now. That's fine. I'll call back in a minute.

Oh no you won't. Oh yes I will.

You shouldn't be calling me at all. I signed up for the Telephone Preference Service (TPS) years ago in order to block this sort of thing. That doesn't really work, I'm afraid. Only about a third of nuisance calls are prevented by TPS.

That's ridiculous. Which is probably why the Information Commissioner's Office(ICO) received 175,000 complaints about unsolicited calls and spam texts last year.

Wow. That's more than Jeremy Clarkson gets. That's because 84% of people surveyed say they've received unsolicited phone calls in the past month. Calls about payment protection insurance alone account for 13% of the total.

Can't someone do something about this modern-day scourge? Up until now, the threshold for legal action has been high. The ICO had to demonstrate that nuisance callers caused "substantial damage or substantial distress". But the government has plans for a crackdown.

How will it work? They want to lower the threshold, making it easier for the ICO to impose fines of up to £500,000 on cold-callers, including high-volume automated recorded messages and texts.

Anything else? The government wants to make it a requirement for all direct marketers to display their phone numbers.

That sounds wonderful, but what can I do to deter cold-callers in the meantime? Stop answering your landline, like the rest of us did years ago. Your mother will figure out how to use Skype eventually.

Do say: "Sylvia's busy – too busy to come to the phone."

Don't say: "A machine that can block 90% of unwanted phone calls? Plus a free iPad mini if I act now? Which button do I press?"

25/05/2015

~ GERBILS ~

Age: Immaterial. Just keep replacing them until your child is old enough to contemplate pet-death with equanimity.

Appearance: Happily, interchangeable.

Oh, gerbils! Cute little snuffly things, racing around their wheels and digging through their sawdust and lapping at their little bottles! So sweet, and so much less of an infinite reproach to existence than goldfish! Yes, until they kill you.

I'm sorry, what? Until they kill you.

I think you might be a bit confused. Are you thinking of lions? If you are, don't worry. Gerbils are a lot smaller and a lot less fierce. You can generally placate them with a sunflower seed. Or is that just hamsters? No, they're vectors for disease. Including the Black Death.

Oh, I see. You're thinking of rats. Black rats spread the Black Death. Well, their fleas did. I read it in Horrible Histories. Wrong, they reckon.

Who reckons? Scientists in Oslo who have just published a study in Proceedings of the National Academy of Sciences purporting to show that while there is no historical correlation between good breeding conditions for rats and the occurrences of plague in the Middle East and Europe, there is between the kind of weather that makes for frisky giant gerbils and millions of bubo-strewn patients all along the Silk Road routes travelled shortly thereafter.

Not my darling Nibbles! He's no harbinger of doom! Wait – did you say giant gerbils? Yes, *Rhombomys opimus*, the great gerbil, found throughout the arid, sandy landscapes of central Asia and a known carrier of the plague pathogen Yersinia pestis.

And how great are these great gerbils? Not great at all for us – did you not hear what I just said about the plague pathogen *Yersinia pestis?*

No, I mean, how big are they? Oh. Up to 8in – or double that if you include the tail.

Wow. What was attractive at one size becomes not at all at another. I know. Like penises.

Mmm. So, are we all safe? As long as one's charming childhood and/or classroom pet doesn't look like something from a James Herbert novel? Yes. Nibbles remains a *Meriones unguiculatus*; the greatest threat is him escaping and gnawing through every electrical wire in the house.

Do say: "Time for your exercise wheel, little one!"

Don't say: "Could I have a packet of sunflower seeds and some aspirin? I'm not feeling so hot."

24/05/2015

~ TOM STOPPARD ~

Name: Tom Stoppard.

Age: 77.

Appearance: Well-lunched Mick Jagger.

Occupation: Don't be silly. You know exactly who he is.

Some sort of writer, isn't he? Our greatest living playwright, to be precise.

The Birthday Party, isn't that one of his? You're thinking of Harold Pinter.

Oh yeah, easily confused. I take it you're not a theatregoer.

I prefer to spend the evening in the pub. You make Sir Tom's point for him.

What point? That audiences are less cultured than they used to be, and that he has to dumb down his allusions accordingly. "Theatregoers have become more ignorant since the 1970s, when playwrights could rely on them to have a basic knowledge of Shakespeare," he complained in a talk at the National Theatre, where his new play The Hard Problem has just opened.

Does he give any examples? Goneril. He referred to her in his play Travesties in 1974, and everyone got it. Then, when the play was revived in 1990, only half the audience knew who she was.

Goneril, Goneril … it rings a bell. Shakespeare is the clue.

Sexually transmitted disease? You may be thinking of Chlamydia – sorry, Calpurnia – in Julius Caesar. Goneril was King Lear's eldest and nastiest daughter.

Ah. Why are dumber audiences a problem for Stoppard? Because his plays are often intertextual. This, after all, is the playwright who found fame almost 50 years ago with Rosencrantz and Guildenstern are Dead. If you don't know which play R&G are from, it doesn't work. Ditto Jumpers, Travesties, After Magritte and The Real Inspector Hound. You need to understand what's being commented on before you can appreciate the play.

They sound too clever for their own good. Funnily enough, you're not the first person to say that.

Did everyone understand The Hard Problem? Only after Stoppard had rewritten one scene three times because preview performances had left audiences bemused.

What's it about? It's about 100 minutes, with no interval.

Did the critics like it? Only the _Daily Mail's_ Quentin Letts.

Oh dear. Yes, unfortunate. Most of the rest found that a play examining consciousness lulled them into a state of unconsciousness.

Do say: "Education isn't what it was in my day."

Don't say: "You don't think it's sour grapes, do you?"

~ THE KEBAB ~

Age: The first recorded use of the word dates to 1377, but this is all fresh today, honest.

Appearance: Sliced lamb or chicken, with salad, inside pitta bread. You want chips with that?

No thanks, I'm far too drunk to eat anything. There's no such thing as too drunk. Only not drunk enough. Try it.

Look, I'm not hungry. I'm angry. And what are you looking at, anyway? Please, take a bite. You'll feel less antisocial.

From eating a kebab? Yes. Especially one from Khans takeaway in Broughty Ferry, Dundee.

Do you have any evidence to support that statement? Just the highly persuasive arguments of solicitor Janet Hood.

Who is she? She's a lawyer representing Khans.

What kind of trouble is Khans in? None. The owners were just applying to the local council for a late-night licence.

And the council opposed it? Some members were worried that the extended hours might lead to antisocial behaviour.

Exactly. Late night takeaways are one-stop shops for antisocial behaviour. They're the opposite, according to Hood.

How so? "Medical evidence strongly suggests that eating after drinking helps induce sleep, which could help lower alcohol-related domestic violence," she said.

I never thought of it that way. She also argued that Khans prevented house fires, by feeding drunks who might otherwise go home and cook.

It sounds likes a fun town, Broughty Ferry. In fact, she claimed, the only trouble caused by Khans came when the post-late-licence-pub crowd turned up and found the place shut.

Give Khans that licence before all hell breaks loose! Don't worry, they did. Khans can now serve food until 2am during the week and 2.30am at weekends. Dozens of other takeaways in the vicinity have also been granted the extension.

Phew! Disaster averted. The council agrees. "I had no idea a kebab could solve so many problems," said one member.

Me neither. They should send kebabs to the Middle East! I think they already have them there.

Yes, but until how late? Good point.

Do say: "Large doner with chilli sauce, please, before I do something I'll regret in the morning."

Don't say: "I'll probably regret eating this in the morning."

31/08/2014

~ LOVE NUGGETS ~

Age: New-fangled.

Appearance: Small, caring, gestural.

That's not really painting much of a picture for me. What are they? Small, caring gestures.

I'm still not quite following you. Give me an example of a "love nugget". Making a cup of tea.

We already have a name for that. It's called "making a cup of tea". More specifically, making a cup of tea, unbidden, for your partner. It's just one of a number of little acts of kindness that can help a relationship thrive.

Interesting. How does it help, exactly? According to the OnePlusOne charity, such small acts "demonstrate commitment, improve communication, show we care, achieve compromise and even resolve conflicts".

All that just from giving someone a cup of tea they probably didn't want in the first place? Other examples include going to the cinema with your partner even though you don't really want to see the film yourself, making creative presents, or giving foot massages.

Sounds pathetic. A study of 4,000 couples found that the most cherished acts of kindness in a relationship tended to be both mundane and spontaneous. Grand gestures were thought far less important.

What if you hate each other? Wouldn't it just be annoying? The idea is to prevent the problems that lead to marital breakdown by keeping your partnership strong. OnePlus One has launched a "love nuggets" campaign, with £45,000 of a £2.7m investment from the Department for Education, to get people to take a more proactive approach to relationships.

That sounds a lot of money. How are they using it? For a start they've launched a website, in partnership with Netmums, dad.info and the Student Room, that includes a "random love nugget generator" to inspire you.

Are you sure? Because I just went and Googled "love nuggets" and found something altogether different. Unfortunately the term does have another, rather less safe-for-work definition.

Absolutely no mention of tea. Yes, I know.

It's a good thing I didn't try to surprise my partner with that one. No. That would have sent the wrong message.

Do say: "Hi Sweetie! Here's that spontaneous cup of tea the government told me to make you."

Don't say: "For future reference, it's two sugars."

28/07/2014

~ THE HAWKING INDEX ~

Age: Brand new!

Appearance: Percentagey.

So it's a percentage? Well I'd say it's really a ratio expressed as a percentage.

Tell me more! Essentially, it shows the average page number of the five most highlighted passages in a Kindle book as a proportion of that book's total length. If a 200-page book's average Kindle highlight appears on page 200, that gives it a Hawking Index (or HI) of 100%. If it's on page 100, 50%. Page 50, 25%. And so on.

I see. Now just remind me why that's interesting. Basically it is supposed to measure how far people get into a book before giving up. The index was flippantly proposed by Jordan Ellenberg, an American mathematician, in a blog for the *Wall Street Journal*. He named it after Stephen Hawking's *A Brief History of Time*.

Cool! So I can see which books everybody buys in order to show off, but then don't actually enjoy? Kind of.

Why only kind of? Oh just because it's statistically flawed. Print readers aren't counted, nor are Kindle-readers who don't use the highlighting feature. And maybe writers put more appealing sentences at the beginning.

Yeah, yeah, yeah. But if we ignore all that? If we ignore all that then this is fun! *Catching Fire*, the second Hunger Games novel, scores 43.4%, which is close to the 50% average you might expect from books that are read to the end. By comparison, the average highlight in *Fifty Shades of Grey* is only 25.9% of the way through it.

It's hard to imagine people buying Fifty Shades in order to show off. It is. But mostly the more prestigious books do have a really low HI – just 6.4% ifor David Foster Wallace's postmodern epic, *Infinite Jest*, for example. And prestigious non-fiction scores still worse. *A Brief History of Time* gets 6.6%, but Thomas Piketty's *Capital in the Twenty-First Century* beats that with 2.4%. (The last of the popular highlights appears on page 26 out of 700.) And Hillary Clinton beats even Piketty. Her new book *Hard Choices* scores just 1.9%!

At what point do people stop reading Pass Notes? Oh, long ago. You can say anything you like now. No one notices.

YOU'RE ALL IDIOTS! Yeah, maybe don't say that.

Do say: "I found Piketty's later chapters especially compelling."

Don't say: "I can't believe Raskolnikov got away with it!"

07/07/2014

~ HILLARY CLINTON ~

Name: Hildebeest.

Age: 66.

Appearance: Coiffed, formidable.

The horns are formidable, I'll grant you that. But I've never seen one looking coiffed. Covered in flies? Yes. Getting eaten by a lioness? Absolutely. Being blow-dried? Not even close. You're thinking of wildebeest. I'm talking about the Hildebeest.

An upland-dwelling subspecies? No. A former US senator and Secretary of State, and a leading contender for the presidency in 2016.

I knew US voters could be a bit eccentric, but I didn't realise they had begun electing ungulates. You misunderstand. The Hildebeest is a nickname for Hillary Clinton.

How horrid! There's such misogyny about first ladies. Who calls Hillary that? Michelle Obama. Allegedly. In a new book called *Blood Feud,* the political journalist Edward Klein says Michelle and her friend Valerie Jarrett love bitching about "the Hildebeest". Indeed, he says that the Clintons and the Obamas hate each other.

But they're the two great Democrat couples – four powerful people with similar interests. How could they possibly fall out? You've answered your own question there. Barack and Hillary were rivals for the Democratic nomination in 2008, during which Klein says the Clinton camp felt unfairly portrayed as racist by the Obamas.

Hey, we're all alleged racists, deep down. Klein claims this is very personal. "I hate that man Obama more than any man I've ever met, more than any man who ever lived," Bill is supposed to have said.

But he endorsed him for reelection in 2012! As part of an alleged deal in which the Obamas are meant to support Hillary's run in 2016. They have to pretend to be friends, and it's dead awkward. During a round of golf, Bill apparently bragged about how much better the economy did in his eight years.

Ooh. When presidents bitch! Barack retorted that Michelle might make a good president one day.

Backatcha! "Bill was speechless," says 'a Clinton family friend'. "If he hadn't been on a mission to strike a deal with Barack, he might have stormed off the golf course then and there." They tried to patch things up at a dinner party in March 2013, but Barack played ostentatiously on his BlackBerry when Bill was talking.

Probably just counting his retweets. No doubt.

Do say: "Ooh, look at me, I'm Barack Obama and I use Twitter and stuff!"

Don't say: "I'm, like, Hillary with two Ls, and I'm desperate to be president even though I'm really annoying!"

23/06/2014

~ JEANETTE WINTERSON ~

Age: 54.

Appearance: Indefatigable.

Oh great – has she written another book? Is that why we're talking about her? Is it a novel or a memoir? I love her. I hope it's a memoir. Or a novel. I really don't mind. She's amazing. She's a murderer.

What? She tweeted "Rabbit ate my parsley. I am eating the rabbit," along with a picture of the disembowelled, semi-skinned, wholly dead rabbit in question lying on her kitchen counter.

Was she the one who actually killed it? Yup. Caught it in a humane trap next to the parsley bed, then did the necessary. Or unnecessary, according to many on Twitter.

Why – do they only follow vegetarians? That's what Winterson said. She also tweeted a picture of her cat eating the entrails and noted that the remaining skin, which includes the head, "makes a great glove puppet".

That seems characteristically provocative. Did it provoke? It did indeed. Some followers were not impressed.

Highlights, please. "Before I unfollow you, you make me sick. I will never again read a word you write. Rest in peace, little rabbit." (Although the tweet used more inventive punctuation).

Harsh. Another said: "How you and your cat have disappoint-ed me! At least the cat has an excuse."

I take it Winterson fought back? She is not known for walking away from a good fight, certainly, and nor did she. She pointed out the hypocrisy of eating farmed supermarket meat then objecting to a picture of something killed by hand that involved "no waste no packaging no processing no food miles". An unrepentant tone was maintained throughout.

She should have said: "My commitment to organic and sustainable living is Written on the Body of this animal." Because she wrote a book called *Written on the Body?*

Yes! Or: "Oranges are Not the Only Fruit that I could braise this rabbit with."Because … yes, I see.

Or "This has become a bit of a Tanglewreck, like my first children's book was called, and my dinner is ready so I'm off." That's enough.

Do say: "Come round for ethically-and-environmentally-sound-comma-irreproachably-principled dinner."

Don't say: "Poor ickle flopsy bunnikins gone all deaded by the bad lady! Pass me my Twitchfork! That is my Twitter pitchfork, btw."

18/06/2014

~ ADORKABLE ~

Age: Seven and a bit.

Appearance: Zooey Deschanel, in a pair of glasses that she doesn't medically need, attempting to give you a friendship bracelet she made but falling on her bottom in the process.

Adorkable? What a horrible word. But it's a real word now. It's in the Collins English Dictionary and everything.

What does it mean? It's a blend of "adorable" and "dork". If you are socially inept in an endearing way, you're adorkable.

So if I wear pink earmuffs to a job interview? You're adorkable!

And if I've ever tried to assemble flatpack furniture with a Hello Kitty toy screwdriver? You're adorkable!

And if I've ever broken into a former partner's house so I could eat their food and sleep in their bed when they were out? It depends. Did you do it while wearing an ironic charity shop jumper?

Sure. You're adorkable!

And this word is in the dictionary because people actually say it out loud? Well, maybe not. Its inclusion is down to the fact that people use it on Twitter a lot, possibly to accompany a picture of a cat in an 1980s headband. There is a chance that the human body would explode with shame if anyone actually said it out loud.

Why is it popular? The first series of the US sitcom New Girl went out of its way to use the word as often as possible in its promotional material back in 2011. There was a backlash, and yet the word endured enough to be used as the title of a 2012 book by Sarra Manning.

Really? What's the book about? According to Amazon: "Jeane Smith's a blogger, a dreamer, a dare-to-dreamer, a jumble sale …"

That's enough. You do know that cutting off synopses of books about adorkable people is not adorkable, don't you?

Why am I starting to think that adorkable is only in the dictionary because it won a competition? Because it did. There was a poll on Twitter, and adorkable won it.

What came second? Felfie: a farmer selfie!

Oh, God. Felfies are adorkable!

Do say: "Your friend over there, absentmindedly picking his nose, is adorkable."

Don't say: "Isn't this just a polite way of saying 'developmentally challenged'?"

10/06/2014

~ KEPLER-10C ~

Age: Maybe nearing its 11 billionth birthday.

Appearance: It's a planet, so it's round. And rocky, we know that. Although with the telescopes and imaging technology currently available it's hard to be utterly precise about these things.

No one's actually seen it, have they? Not "seen it" as such. But scientists at the Harvard-Smithsonian Center for Astrophysics have just announced that they know it's there.

How exactly? Because Kepler-10c blocks some of its sun's light when it moves past it. Nasa's Kepler space telescope, from which the planet gets its name, is good at noticing these things. It has already found hundreds of other distant planets.

We all have our talents. I can almost bake bread. Good for you. Although Kepler-10c is about 560 lightyears from Earth, and that's about 3,293 trillion miles, so I think spotting that's more impressive. It's also MASSIVE.

Oh yes? How big is it? A little more than twice the width of Earth.

Not bad. Although if I'm honest I was kind of hoping for more than that. Ah, but size isn't the point here. I said it's "massive" – about 17 times the mass of Earth. Those scientists reckon the gravity of all that mass has squashed it together, making it very dense indeed – around 7.5g/cc. That's a bit like being made of solid iron.

Cool! Exactly. The scientists announced its discovery on Tuesday, and have declared a new class of planet for it – the mega-Earth. Until now, no one knew that rocky planets could get so massive. "This is the Godzilla of Earths!" said Professor Dimitar Sasselov. "But unlike the movie monster, Kepler-10c has positive implications for life."

I love it when scientists do jokes. We all do. Although Sasselov was making another point about 10c's coolness. It means that there are more rocky planets out there than was thought, which means there are more places where aliens might live. Indeed if 10c has clouds it might even be cool enough to sustain life itself.

So there could be mega-Earthlings! Let's not go nuts.

Do say: "I want to go there!"

Don't say: "Even the fastest spacecraft that mankind has ever built would take more than 10,000 years to travel to Kepler-10c so, at best, it could perhaps deliver your corpse."

03/06/2014

~ LE TRAIN ~

Age: Very new.

Appearance: At a standstill.

Le train. Let me guess – French trains are in the news? Quel cleverness, mon petit chou! Yes, they are.

Et pourquoi? Because the French train company SNCF just took delivery of the 2,000 new trains it ordered at a cost of £12.1bn and discovered that they are too wide for more than 1,000 regional stations.

Merde! How did that happen? Apparently the national rail operator RFF gave SNCF the wrong dimensions.

Ha! I _knew_ nobody really understood the metric system! What excuse did RFF give? "Your Nigel Farage et your Charles de Prince are right – it is une système inhumain!" No. Rather, they seem to have measured only the width of platforms less than 30 years old. Those more than 50 years old – like most of the stations in rural areas – were built when trains were slightly smaller.

So the stations d'un certain age went unnoticed? Invisible to men, were they? Quelle surprise! Typique! It's more typical of the kind of mistakes and inefficiency you find when you separate the rail operators from the train companies.

What are you basing that statement on? The words of monsieur Frederic Cuvillier, a junior transport minister. "When you separate the rail operator from the train company," he said, "this is what happens."

But think of the money a few people wouldn't make if you allowed them to stay together, working in unison

for the efficient transportation of passengers rather than the financial gain of shareholders! You fool. Hmm, yes, sorry.

So, what are they going to do about this grande fuque-up? Claim the grinding action of the trains against the platforms is a subtly erotic pleasure befitting the national character, I suppose? No. They have begun work to widen the thousand-plus stations affected. So far, the whole thing has cost more than £40m.

That's very nearly the cost of an annual London travelcard zones 1-6! Vraiment.

This could be their Waterloo! And we're done.

Do say: "Ils sont magnifiques, mais ils ne sont pas going to fit."

Don't say: "Well, this rather puts the mockers on the forthcoming book Why French Trains Don't Get Fat, doesn't it?"

21/05/2014

~ GLOCKER MOMS ~

Age: Varies.

Appearance: Terrifying.

What's so scary about a suburban mother who works hard for her children? You're thinking of soccer moms. These are Glocker Moms. They are basically the same, except they own a gun and hate liberals.

As in Glock, the renowned Austrian handgun manufacturer? You catch on fast.

This sounds to me like an American thing. Right again.

The National Rifle Association (NRA) claims that a quarter of the attendees at its recent annual meeting in Indianapolis were women, up from, at best, 5-10% a decade ago. It also put a huge poster of a female gun activist on the front of the building and handed out "I'm an NRA MOM" badges on the door.

It must be very pleased with this development. Yes, pleased. And also probably keen to make the most of it. On the one hand, more American women do seem to be developing a love of guns. The number of female-held gun permits in Indiana, for instance, has risen by almost 43% in the past two years, and there are certainly more pink guns, targets and holsters on the market.

What sane woman wouldn't want one of those? Indeed. On the other hand, gun manufacturers, which supply much of the NRA's funding, need to appeal to women and minorities to find future growth. Plus this is a very convenient riposte to Moms Demand Action for Gun Sense in America, a growing group of anti-gun activists that sprang up following the Sandy Hook massacre.

Good idea. Bad name. That's your opinion. But they are not to be trifled with, despite their peaceful nature.

Why would lots of women suddenly want a gun anyway? Mostly for protection from men, they say. Although statistics show that women with access to firearms-sare much more likely to become homicide victims – and to a greater extent than male gun-owners.

Perhaps it's just that they don't have quite enough guns yet? The US already owns vastly more guns per person, as well as having a higher rate of gun deaths, than any other developed country.

What about giving every household their own vat of anthrax? Have they tried that? Sounds like a great idea.

Do say: "The rate of gun deaths in the US is more than 40 times higher than in the UK."

Don't say: "Do your homework, punk!"

07/05/2014

~ THE BANTER SQUADRON ~

Age: Unknown.

Appearance: Secretive. But probably not too hard to spot.

The Banter Squadron? The Banter Squadron? That sounds like something a heinous bunch of pricks would call themselves. Go on.

Maybe it's just me, but it conjures up a vision of a small gang of arrogant, self-regarding young – I'm going to go out on a limb here and say men – swanning around, stinking up the place with an air of smug overprivilege and entitlement while drinking and making each other laugh with non-witticisms they mistakenly regard as banter. And where might this place be?

If I had to guess, I'd say Oxbridge. Or, if there's a difference, Westminster. Well done. They're an elite secret drinking society in Oxford. They're also known as the Red Trouser Brigade.

And the hits just keep on coming. Why are we giving them newspaper and brain space? Because the president of the Oxford Union tried to secure union funds in order to sue a student newspaper after it outed him as a member.

Oxford toff gets narked by Oxford thing being talked about by other Oxford thing at Oxford. Why do I care? Perhaps because it gives us a window on to the formative years of so many of the people who have governed and who are currently governing our lives.

Like who? Recent former presidents of the Union include Michael Heseltine, William Hague, Damian Green, Michael Gove, Boris Johnson … I could go on.

Please don't. Former members of elite drinking societies include – in the Bullingdon Club alone – John Profumo, Alan Clark, David Cameron, George Osborne, Jo and Boris Johnson … I could, again, go on.

Please, again, don't. It's terrifying. Terrifying to realise from what a small pool our politicians are drawn from, or terrifying to realise what kind of forces, activities and tastes shaped them in their youth?

Both. It makes me think of a nest of baby eels slithering over and over each other … And eventually knotting themselves into a slimy, glutinous, inextricable mass?

Yes. If eels could wear red trousers and burn £50 notes in front of homeless people, I think you'd have it in one.

Do say: "Up the revolution"

Don't say: "Tony Benn, Philip Toynbee and Paul and Michael Foot were Union presidents too, you revisionist commie bastards!"

02/05/2014

~ HAND-ME-UPS ~

Name: Hand-me-ups.

Age: Well past it.

Appearance: Clapped-out antique.

Like a rusting Morris Minor? No, like an iPhone 4S.

But that's the sort of phone I have. You surprise me, old man.

What's wrong with it? It does everything I need it to do, and more. Why, it's like a watch and a walkie talkie in one! How many pixels does the camera have?

There's a camera in it? Has it got fast wireless? 64-bit architecture? Fingerprint recognition?

I don't really know that much about it, to be honest. One of my kids gave it to me when he got an upgrade. That's why it's called a hand-me-up, granddad.

Sorry, what's that? According to a new study from an online retailer, old technology − including phones, tablets, TVs − are increasingly being "handed up" to parents by their children. Apparently one in three UK mums is now using a phone handed up by another family member.

Sounds very sensible. The older generation − that's you − isn't really concerned with having the most up-to-date stuff, whereas people under 25 tend to think a smartphone needs replacing after 11 months.

That's ridiculous − just because the screen is a bit scratched and it sometimes plays loud music in your pocket for no reason. It's still perfectly serviceable. It's all yours, mate.

You young people wouldn't know you were born if you didn't have an app to remind you it was your birthday. Such mindless consumption. Actually, hand-me-ups are a pretty efficient form of recycling: new technology enters the household through the family member most concerned with novelty, and ends up with the person who cares least, extending the lifespan of the product.

Do you know that if my children ring me, their names and faces actually appear on the screen? It was nice talking to you. You take care now.

Before you go, could you just show me how to get Radio 4 on it? I'm late as it is. Bye.

Do say: "Like me, this old phone may be cracked and obsolete, but there's plenty of life left in both of us."

Don't say: "When I was your age we had to crush our own candy, with a mallet."

25/04/2014

~ PALCOHOL ~

Age: Weeks old, regulation-wise.

Appearance: Illicit-looking white powder.

Is it illicit? Not at all. In fact it's been approved for sale by the US Alcohol and Tobacco Tax and Trade Bureau.

And what is it, exactly? It's powderised alcohol.

Come again? It's alcohol in powder form. Just add water.

You mean it turns water into wine? It turns water into either vodka or rum, or optional flavours including cosmopolitan, mojito and the Powderita – a powdered margarita.

Move over, Jesus! There's a new miracle worker in town! There is indeed: Mark Phillips, inventor of Palcohol.

Tell me more about him. "Mark is an active guy," according to the Palcohol website. "After hours of an activity, he sometimes wanted to relax and enjoy a refreshing adult beverage."

You know who Mark reminds me of? Me! Mark didn't want to carry bulky bottles of alcohol on his activities, so he invented Palcohol. But it has loads of other handy applications.

Really? I can't think of any. What about adding it to food for an extra kick?

Rum on your cornflakes? The Palcohol website suggested vodka on eggs, but it's the same idea – drinking at breakfast "to start your day off right".

Great thinking! What other advice does the website have? It suggested taking Palcohol into expensive venues to jazz up soft drinks, and mentioned "the elephant in the room".

Which is what? The already high rates of alcohol-related disease in the US? No – "snorting Palcohol".

Can you? Apparently you can, but you shouldn't.

They shouldn't have put the idea in my head, then. To be fair, all that advice came from a part of the website that was "experimenting with some humorous and edgy verbiage about Palcohol". It wasn't meant to be public, and it's since been removed. They've also added "volume" to the powder to make snorting it more trouble than it's worth.

Do they have any revised suggestions? Only that you consume Palcohol responsibly, and treat it the way you would any other form of alcohol.

I can't do both - which is it?

Do say: "Take your Pal wherever you go!"

Don't say: "Stranded in the desert? Use Palcohol to turn your urine into beer!"

21/04/2014

~ 5G ~

Age: Minus two years.

Appearance: Look, over there! You missed it. Now it's over there! Too late. Quick, now it's … no, it's gone again.

Are you trying to say that 5G is fast? That's exactly what I'm trying to say. You know 4G?

The thing that gives you internet on your phone? Yes, that's right. Well, forget 4G. 4G's old hat. David Cameron has just announced a deal to develop 5G technology with Germany, and it's going to be 1,000 times faster than 4G.

Oh. My phone still only goes up to 3G. 3G? What are you, some sort of loser? How long does it take you to download a film to your phone?

I don't really download films to my phone. I mainly just use it for Facebook and Angry Bir … One second! That's how quickly you can download a film on 5G. In the time it took me to tell you that, I could have downloaded every film that Michael Bay ever made. Pow!

What's the benefit of that? Who genuinely needs to

download a film in less than a second? People with … people who want to … oh, look, I don't know. But it sounds cool, right?

This isn't just about films, is it? Nope. Cameron says he wants the UK to be the most digital nation in the G8, and this is simply a step towards achieving that.

What did he say exactly? "Countries like the UK and Germany will only succeed if we have a relentless drive for new ideas and innovations".

And unnecessarily fast mobile internet is one of those innovations. Yes. But he's also investing £73m in The Internet of Things.

Wait, the what? I'm confused. Isn't the internet already a thing? For now. Soon it will be our pulsating sentient overlord that feasts on the blood of the young but, look, we'll worry about that when we have to.

So what's the Internet of Things? In the future, your watch will take your blood pressure and then tell your fridge to preventatively buy in vegetables and probiotic yoghurt, because the things you own know you better than you know yourself. That's the Internet of Things.

I want to go and live in a cave. A whole film in one second! Pow!

Do say: "5G is the future of technology."

Don't say: "Until 6G comes along, at which point you'll be made to feel like a failure for only having 5G."

10/03/2014

~ THE CLING-ONS ~

Name: The Cling-ons

Age: They're a relatively recent phenomenon.

Appearance: Stressed people.

I already know all about them. You do?

Don't sound so surprised. I've studied their ways. I even speak their language. It's just that the term was only coined a few days ago by the FT ...

"Heghlu'meH QaQ jajvam!" That means: "Today is a good day to die!" I think we might be talking about two different sorts of Cling-on.

I doubt it. Well, I'm talking about a particular subset of high-earning professionals who are finding it increasingly hard to "cling on" to the trappings of middle-class life.

I see. Do they have deeply ridged foreheads? Not exclusively, no. They're largely academics, scientists, architects and engineers.

Ah, yes. Different Cling-ons. Yours sound less warlike and better paid. They used to be. In the 70s such professionals earned more than people who worked in the City, but now they're struggling to make ends meet. These days an academic makes £48K on average, a natural scientist just £42K.

Where I come from £42K is a lot of money. What planet are you on, Mr Cling-on scientist? That sort of salary doesn't stretch very far in the south-east, where the Cling-ons have been outstripped in earnings by an über-middle class – doctors, lawyers and financial-services workers – who are driving up school fees and house prices.

What are the implications, if any? It means that London is increasingly a no-go area for the ordinary middle classes, and that even those who study science and engineering tend to look for jobs in the financial sector after graduation.

Why don't the scientists and academics just kill all the bankers and lawyers, lay waste to their workplaces and colonise their expensive properties? Because they're not that kind of Klingon, remember?

Oh yeah. So what can be done? Hard to say, but it certainly presents a challenge for policymakers, if we don't want certain academic qualifications to become economically unfeasible, and our capital city to become a bankers' ghetto.

Do say: "Unless we address the high disparity in earnings among the middle classes, these so-called Cling-ons will be driven into our poorest regions and neighbourhoods."

Don't say: "Here they come. Set phasers to stun."

25/03/2015

~ CAMERON DIAZ ~

Age: 41.

Appearance: Ridiculously beautiful, of course. She's a film star.

What's she up to? Usual stuff: appearing in movies, treading the red carpet, having sex with a car.

Eh? Having sex with a car in her new film, The Counselor, which is released this week in the UK.

I'm joining the queue now. It'll probably be short. The film flopped in the US.

But Cameron Diaz has sex with a car! What sort of car is it? Have a guess.

Austin Allegro? No.

Nissan Bluebird? You're not taking this seriously.

Skoda Fabia? Idiot. It's a yellow Ferrari California. Diaz climbs on to the windscreen, and – how do I put this delicately?

Are you blushing? Well, let's just say that she, well, stays on the windscreen until she has an orgasm, while her boyfriend, played by Javier Bardem, watches in terror from the driver's seat.

Did Diaz do the whole scene herself? There are rumours of a stunt double.

Sounds pretty demeaning for them both. Well, apparently – according to one analysis – the scene could be seen as a metaphor of female empowerment. Malkina, the Barba-dian-born drug dealer played by Diaz, is demonstrating she doesn't need men. For anything.

Righto. Where was the scene shot? Colombia? Mexico? LA? No. At Stoke Park golf course in Buckinghamshire.

And you say the film failed at the box office in the US? Too dark and amoral, apparently. The 90 seconds of absurd, attention-grabbing sex were not enough to offset the two hours of talky tedium in Cormac McCarthy's screenplay. The script's gems include the aphorism: "The truth has no temperature."

Profound. Doesn't Diaz have form when it comes to dodgy sex scenes? You're thinking of the carwash scene in Bad Teacher, which may well have inspired the mechaphilia in The Counselor. Not to mention the hair gel scene in There's Something About Mary.

Not to be confused with: Dame Judi Dench.

Do say: "Sounds like a turkey – on wheels."

Don't say: "Nice car, want to show me what it can do?"

10/11/2013

~ MICK JAGGER ~

Age: 69.

Appearance: Dorian Gray's portrait trying to walk across a rope bridge in a gale.

Finally, we get to shake up Pass notes with some old-fashioned rock'n'roll rebellion. What has Jagger got up to this time? Sex? Drugs? Close. He's just publicly declared his admiration for Margaret Thatcher.

Ironically, right? Like when Brian Jones dressed up as a Nazi? No. Unironically, like when the Nazis dressed up as Nazis.

Fine. What did he say about her? "In the 80s or early 90s I met her a couple of times. I don't want to talk about what we talked about, especially now that everybody else is blabbing about her."

But? "But ... I was slightly surprised by all the people that were still so anti her and had all this residual resentment."

What? Mick Jagger is a secret Conservative? Who knew? Well, in fairness, probably everyone.

Just because he's a knight of the realm? How disgustingly classist of you. There's that, and there's his policy of charging so much for Rolling Stones tickets that you pretty well need to own a top hat and monocle to get in.

The man's got to make a living, you know. What other proof of this secret conservatism do you have? Rush Limbaugh loves him for refusing to give anyone – including his own kids – a financial leg-up.

You can't start using Rush Limbaugh as a sensible

political yardstick. Is that really all you've got? There's also his 1987 single Let's Work. The one about how much Mick Jagger hates people on benefits. The one that goes: "Ain't gonna sweat for you/ Ain't gonna cry for you/ If you're lazy."

Lalalalalala. I can't hear you. It's fine. Calm down. Lots of other cool celebrities liked Margaret Thatcher. Phil Collins. Jeremy Clarkson. Jimmy Savile ...

At least there's still Keith Richards. He's still proof that the anti-establishment fire of rock'n'roll will never die. The same Keith Richards who ended his autobiography with a lovely recipe for bangers and mash?

Oh, for God's sake. Sorry.

Do say: "Play Sympathy for the Devil!"

Don't say: "Play Ding Dong the Witch is Dead!"

13/06/2013

~ JAPANESE KNOTWEED ~

Age: Immortal.

Appearance: Unstoppable.

Just looks like a weed to me. It's *fallopia japonica*! Accursed invader of our gentle homeland! Fearsome coloniser of peaceful lands! Bringer of ecological Armageddon to our hapless shores. Damn you! Damn you all to hell!

That seems a bit harsh. A weed is just a weed. Do you get this worked up about dandelions? Dandelions are as the most rare and precious orchids compared to this barbaric thing.

It can't be that bad. It grows everywhere. More specifically, it grows through everywhere. Concrete foundations. Expensively laid and maintained roads. Flood defences. Walls. And kills off every indigenous species, every flower, every delicately calibrated nearby ecosystem. All brutalised by a virtually indestructible root system.

Yikes! And now – and now, it has reached the celebrity homes of Hampstead, north London.

No! Yes! Tom Conti, Thierry Henry, Esther Rantzen and Melanie Sykes are all under threat from an infestation.

What can we do to help? Not much. A benefit gala would take too long. One of the main reasons it's classed as one of the hundred most invasive species on the planet by the World Conservation Union is that it can grow 10cm a day.

This is terrifying! I know. That's why the UK spends more than £150m a year fighting it. We have even passed laws against it.

Was that not energy wasted? Or can this thing read statutes too? No, the Wildlife and Countryside Act 1981 made it an offence for anyone to "plant or otherwise cause [it] to grow in the wild".

Ah, that makes more sense. And it is classed as controlled waste under the Environmental Protection Act 1990. You have to dispose of it at special landfill sites.

Well, someone left a stray node somewhere. Perhaps we could all chip in for some psyllid bugs.

What are they? Hallucinogens? Just let Conti et al party to forget their worries? They're knotweed's natural enemy. Defra announced plans a few years ago to introduce them to save our fair isle from strangulation.

I'm on it. Ebay, don't fail me now.

Do say: "Slash! Burn! Don't worry, Thierry, I'll save you."

Don't say: "At the end of the book, they never actually defeated the Triffids, did they?

09/06/2013

~ GLENN CLOSE ~

Age: 66.

Appearance: Regal glamour; occasional outbursts of bowler-hatter androgyny.

Another Fatal Attraction star in the news this week? Oh God, does this mean ... No, you're safe. She hasn't suddenly revealed that she caught anything from oral sex. This is a cunnilingus-free zone. But she does want to apologise.

For Fatal Attraction? Good, justice for that poor rabbit is long overdue. This has nothing to do with bunny boiling.

Then why is she apologising? Is it her gigantic perm? Oh, be quiet, it was the 80s. We all looked like that back then. No, Close wishes to apologise for her insensitive portrayal of mental illness in the film.

Go on. She regrets playing up to the pervasive negative stereotypes of the day. "Most people with mental illness are not violent," she told CBS News. "And most people who commit violent crimes do not have a diagnosed mental illness. That is wrong, and it's proven wrong and it is immoral to keep that perpetrated."

What? You mean to say that not everyone with a mental

illness ends up trying to stab Michael Douglas in his bathroom? Pretty much not a single person with mental illness has ever tried to stab Michael Douglas in his bathroom. Astonishing, isn't it?

Out of interest, did we ever learn what type of mental illness Glenn Close's character had? Apparently it was Clérambault's syndrome, a form of paranoid delusion based on the false assumption that a figure of admiration is in love with them, although Close maintains that this was never discussed during production.

Clérambault's syndrome, eh? Sounds weird. Listen, you're the one talking to yourself. At least Close is conscientious enough to finally speak out about this after such a long time.

You're right. Hey, while she's at it, can she apologise for 102 Dalmatians as well? Because she played Cruella De Vil's manic tendencies for laughs?

No, because it wasn't very good. Well, I suppose that's only fair.

Do say: "More actors should sensitively examine the underlying motivations of their characters."

Don't say: "This is all well and good, but it's hardly going to bring that poor rabbit back to life."

05/06/2013

~ VIAGRA ~

Age: First brought to market in 1998. So 15.

Appearance: Little blue pill.

There's Viagra news? There is indeed.

What's up now? Guess.

The company's performing better? Nope.

Stockholders are experiencing unprecedented growth? Not exactly.

There has been a healthy rise in the share price? Guess again.

This is too hard. I give up. Viagra manufacturer Pfizer is about to lose its patent protection in the UK.

You mean the effects of the patent are wearing off? More or less. The patent expires on 21 June. Rival companies will then be free to sell generic versions of the drug – which is commonly used to treat erectile dysfunction – under its chemical name, sildenafil.

Can't these Pfizer guys just take another one? Another patent? No. Patents don't work like that. Once they're gone, they're gone.

So UK sales are about to flop? Perhaps. Estimates suggest as many as 20 manufacturers plan to unveil generic versions of sildenafil in the next few months, at prices more than 10 times lower than the current rate of around £10 a pill.

And without the patent, Pfizer won't be able to keep it up? Probably not, no. Sildenafil may soon be on shelves for as little as 85p a pill. Which is good news not just for users but for the taxpayer as well. The NHS spent around £40m on Viagra in 2012 and could be set to make major savings if doctors choose to prescribe a cheaper alternative.

How does Pfizer feel about all of this? Embarrassed and powerless? Not entirely. The drug is still making the company around $2bn a year and it plans to stay in on the action here in the UK by launching its own cut-price alternative, Sildenafil Pfizer, when the patent runs out. Plus, it still has another seven years until the patent wears off in America.

So they can keep going at it with US customers until 2020? Pretty much.

Do say: "Don't worry about it. It happens to most enormous pharmaceutical companies."

Don't say: "I just never thought it would happen to an enormous pharmaceutical company like me."

03/06/2013

~ GRUMPY CAT ~

Age: 1.

Appearance: Take a wild guess.

OK, I'm picturing a cat. Yes.

But it looks – how can I put this? – almost disgruntled. There you go.

What a funny idea! Many people think so. And this is a real cat. Her name is Tardar Sauce (a misspelling of tartar sauce, which she was said to resemble), and she lives with the Bundesen family in Arizona. She looks grumpy because her mouth is slightly deformed by a genetic disorder.

Hilarious! It's essentially a type of feline dwarfism, which also restricts the mobility of her back legs.

Stop! Stop! I'm going to wet myself! Grumpy Cat first came to public attention last September when Bryan Bundesen, the brother of her owner Tabatha, posted a photograph of her on Reddit. Further photographs and videos followed, to which people added captions, and Grumpy Cat became...

An internet sensation? I'm afraid so. To date, the Bundesen family have made more than $100,000 from book deals, drinks tie-ins, merchandising and public appearances. There may be a Grumpy Cat movie now as well.

Really? Yes. Ben Lashes, Grumpy Cat's agent, has just sold an option to Broken Road Productions. "We think we can build a big family comedy around this character," says the boss, Todd Garner.

Sorry, Grumpy Cat has an agent? That's right. Lashes is a specialist in making money out of the image rights of cats that become popular on the internet.

And that's a job now, is it? Yup. He started out with Keyboard Cat, then took on Nyan Cat and Princess Monster Truck.

Princess what? She's a cat. That's her name. She has an absurdly pronounced underbite. "When it comes to cats, Ben knows who is going to be big," says Nyan Cat's creator, Christopher Torres.

Do you ever wake up feeling like the world got weird overnight? Daily.

Do say: "Hey, if I was being ritually mocked by millions of people, I'd be grumpy too."

Don't say: "There needs to be a *Guardian* Cat."

~ JEREMY IRONS ~

Age: 64.

Appearance: The Ghost of Fassbender Future.

The actor? Yes, that Jeremy Irons. The one with an Oscar and a penchant for bold political statements.

Such as? Describing smokers as "a minority that cannot speak back", worthy of the same protection as "handicapped people and children". Or calling the fox-hunting ban "one of the two most devastating parliamentary votes in the last century". Or arguing: "If a man puts his hand on a woman's bottom, any woman worth her salt can deal with it."

Classy. And what has he done now? Voiced a truly bizarre objection to gay marriage.

How bizarre are we talking here? Extremely, utterly and bafflingly. As bizarre as a bursar at a bazaar buying basalt for Bashar al-Assad. So bizarre it can be seen from space.

What did he say? "Tax-wise, it's an interesting one, because, you see, could a father not marry his son?"

I'm sorry? It's exactly as it sounds. Jeremy Irons is worried dads will marry their sons. For tax reasons.

Does he think that mums marry their sons for tax reasons at the moment? No, of course he doesn't.

Because? Because there are laws against that kind of thing.

He doesn't think there might also be very similar laws against marriages between fathers and sons? How could there be?

How could there *not* be? Because, as Irons went on to

explain: "It's not incest between men. Incest is there to protect us from inbreeding. But men don't breed, so incest wouldn't cover that. So if I wanted to pass on my estate without death duties I could marry my son and pass on my estate to him."

Ah, faultless legal reasoning. He's clearly given this a lot of thought. Well, he is a thoughtful guy. He went on to explain he was speaking as "a man who has a dog that he loves", and added: "Living with another animal – whether it be a husband or a dog – is great."

Do say: "There's a rumour Jeremy Irons wants to marry his dog ..."

Don't say: "... he says for love, the dog says for tax reasons."

05/04/2013

~ CAROLINE KENNEDY ~

Age: 55.

Appearance: JFK's daughter.

Who is she? JFK's daughter. Also: an attorney, editor, fundraiser and philanthropist.

And what is she up to now? She is finally getting involved in the family business.

Being ludicrously rich? No, she has been in that for ages. The other family business.

Tragic deaths? Again, no, and that is not really a business. Not a viable one anyway.

What then? American politics.

Ah, that. Now that is a business. Is she running for the Senate or for Congress? Neither. She is not running for anything, in fact. She is, however, being vetted for the job of US ambassador to Japan.

Does that mean she has been offered it? Yup, and she is expected to announce that she will accept the role as soon as the selection panel are satisfied that being the daughter of a former president doesn't mean she is some kind of spy or robot.

So why her? Because diplomacy runs in the family. Her grandfather Joe was once ambassador to the UK, and her aunt Jean was Bill Clinton's ambassador to Ireland.

But does she have any kind of Japanese expertise? Nope, not at all.

Or, say, experience in politics? Not a huge amount, no.

Specifically, one disastrous flirtation when she ran for a seat in the Senate five years ago. The would-be campaign – described by the Washington Post as "a surreal train wreck" – came off the tracks almost immediately when critics seized upon her verbal tic of repeating the words "you know" as evidence of a lack of political nous.

Was that a bit harsh? Well, you know, she did, you know, use the phrase 138 times in an interview with the *New York Times* and, you know, 168 times in a half-hour interview with NY One, including, at one point, four times in the same, you know, sentence.

Wow. That is intensely annoying. I know. Imagine how it sounds in Japanese.

Do say: "It's, you know, not who, you know, you know, it's what, you know, you know..."

Don't say: "... and also who, you know, knows you, or knows your, you know, famous family.

02/04/2013

~ GARY GOLDSMITH ~

Age: 47.

Appearance: Un-regal.

Full name: Gary Goldsmith.

Motto: "It's Gary's world, you just live in it."

Occupation: Self-made IT-recruitment millionaire, but better known as the dodgy/maverick (delete according to taste) brother of Carole Middleton, and thus uncle of the saintly Kate.

Ah, yes, wasn't there a spot of bother just before her wedding to William? Indeed. Goldsmith was the victim of a *News of the World* sting in which he allegedly offered undercover reporters drugs and Brazilian prostitutes at his lovely home in Ibiza.

It happens. How did the Middletons react? Initially with fury, but they eventually relented, and he was allowed to attend the wedding.

How did it go? Splendidly. He kept a low profile, arriving in a £280,000 bright blue Rolls-Royce Phantom convertible.

Has he been keeping his nose clean since? He's a reformed character, staying away from the nightclubs he used to frequent on Ibiza, marrying for a fourth time, and even turning La Maison de Bang Bang into a centre for alternative therapies.

La Maison de Bang Bang? That's what his house on Ibiza is called. Critics say it's a reference to sex; he insists it alludes to the island's music scene.

So he's back in favour? Well, he was until this week.

What's happened? He has given an interview to Hello! magazine, discreetly tucked across 16 pages, describing Kate and William's stays at La Maison de Bang Bang.

Oh no! Not drugs, lapdancers, Brazilian prostitutes? Sadly not. Mud baths, DJing and swimming in the pool.

So what's the problem? Well, it still looks like he's cashing in on his royal niece, especially at a time when he's put La Maison de Bang Bang up for sale.

So Hello! could be Goodbye! Probably not. He and Carole, who were raised in a council house in Middlesex, are close, and Kate is said to regard him as a "lovable rogue". "He's obviously a colourful character but the royal family has plenty of black sheep of its own," says royal watcher Jennie Bond sagely.

Not to be confused with: Princess Anne.

Most likely to say: "I've got my own rooms at Buckingham Palace, the Goldsmith Wing! I'm going to be the Duke of Slough!"

Least likely to say: "No comment."

19/03/2013

~ LEFTOVERS ~

Age: Variable

Appearance: Not at their best

Ooh, leftovers! Best meal of the day! Roast beef sandwiches! Whizzed up into soups! Jammed indiscriminately on a plate and warmed up in the microwave, bacterial risk be damned! You're right, but I'm talking about a different kind of leftover.

Really? What kind. The woman kind.

I already don't like where this is going. Nor should you, painfully liberal sir, nor should you. "Leftovers" is apparently how the state refers to refer to women in China who remain unmarried after the age of 25.

Yikes! That's – well, yikes! I know. And they're not alone in their deployment of base terminology for the phenomenon of women deemed by their sociocultural milieu to be past their marriageable peak.

How so? The people of the Philippines refer to women of 30-plus as "over the calendar" – ie exceeding the number of days in a month.

Basically, denoting a number and age so vast as to be unrecordable and virtually inconceivable? Quite so. For those moments when "past it" doesn't seem quite enough. And in Japan, the term in use is "Christmas cakes".

Don't tell me – unsold after 25? Correct. What a way you have with the derogatory pun, sir.

It's just a gift. Now, I feel I must ask the obvious question – do any of these cultures have similarly objectionable

words for unmarried men of a certain age? Unmarried Chinese men over are known as "bare branches". Which is quite nice. But they are in surplus because of the preference for sons under the one-child policy and high abortion rate of female foetuses.

So the cavalcade of damning proof of the intractable nature of patriarchal prejudice and misogyny never really falters then? No. Of course, I feel I must point out that we, the British, are hardly blameless in this regard. "Spinster" and "old maid" are unlovely words for unlovely attitudes, while the equivalent, "bachelor", has always connoted life of fun and freedom.

They're still better than a state-sanctioned comparison to discarded food, though, aren't they? I'll give you that, yes. I'll give you that.

Do say: Up yours. I'm a magnificent main course.

Don't say: Marry me! Whoever you are, just marry me, please!

24/02/2013

~ EMIRATES AIR LINE ~

Age: Eight months.

Appearance: White elephant.

Don't you mean whizzy, state-of-the-art cable car masterminded by Londonmayor Boris Johnson and sponsored by the Emirates airline? I know exactly what I mean.

You are talking about the cable car across the River Thames in east London linking Greenwich Peninsula and the Royal Docks? Yes, that's the one.

Marvellous. I took Freddie and Jemima on it during the Olympics and they adored it. That may be the problem. It fitted perfectly with the boisterous mood of Jubolympics London and was getting up to 70,000 users a week, but numbers are now down to 16,000 and critics are starting to question its future.

Cynics! That's what Boris reckons. "They said the Victoria Line and the Docklands Light Railway would be empty. Give it time."

How long? At least until he's become PM.

Why are numbers falling? Boris blames strong winds, which have led to temporary closures. But that's just hot air. The real problem is it's a tourist attraction rather than the commuter service he originally trumpeted, and will only be viable in peak holiday seasons.

Where are the regular users? They barely exist. The number of commuters using it has been estimated at 16. It would have been cheaper to buy them a gold-plated mini-bus.

Is it losing money? An estimated £50,000 a week.

Somebody must find it useful. It's quite handy for anyone north of the river who wants to go to Tesco Express in Greenwich.

What's the solution? Move it.

Where? Switzerland.

You'd better supply a few basic facts to fill up the rest of the space. Cost £60m to build (more than double the original estimate); Emirates is providing £36m in sponsorship over 10 years; 1,150m long, 90m high, with 34 cabins capable of carrying 5,000 people an hour; fare £4.30 or £3.20 if you pay by Oyster; journey lasts five minutes.

Not to be confused with: The Humber Bridge – another pointless project built for spurious reasons connecting two places no one wants to go to.

Do say: "You get a wonderful view ...

Don't say: "... of the O2 car park."

18/02/2013

~ URBAN FOXES ~

Age: Life expectancy is less than two years.

Appearance: Foxy.

What's the difference between an urban fox and a regular fox? It is largely a question of postcode. Many foxes move between town and country, and most urban foxes are, in fact, suburban. Generally speaking, a fox is a fox.

Wrong! Urban foxes are marauding giants that feed on takeaway curries, cats and babies. That image is more urban myth than urban fox.

But one just attacked a baby in south-east London! True, but such incidents are rare, according to the RSPCA. Foxes only attack out of fear, and tend to shy away from humans and larger animals.

But they also get huge from eating KFC out of bins! Some are the size of horses! Urban foxes aren't bigger than rural foxes, and they mostly don't eat out of bins. The main reason they go near houses is because people feed them.

And that's why the population is exploding! We're overrun! There isn't any hard evidence for that – the last estimate, from the 1980s, put the total urban population at 33,000. The consensus among experts is that there has been no significant increase since, largely because populations are still recovering from a mange epidemic. Numbers may, of course, fluctuate locally.

Well, the mayor of London, Boris Johnson, described them as a "menace", and I can't see that they do any good. They do eat a lot of rats. Who knows what London's rodent problem would be like without 10,000 urban foxes patrolling the streets.

I say we cull them all and find out. Culls don't work. New foxes move straight into unoccupied territory, and they also breed too rapidly to make extermination effective. Fox populations are, in fact, remarkably self-regulating.

Can we just trap them and move them to the country? The country doesn't really want them, and, anyway, they tend to come back.

Do say: "We must strive to understand this noble creature, while keeping our wheelie bins shut tight."

Don›t say: "Hello, Mr Fox! Would you like half a pasta salad?

11/02/2013"

~ BEYONCÉ ~

Age: 31.

Appearance: Uncannily similar to Beyoncé.

You mean *the* Beyoncé? Are there other Beyoncés?

I don't know. I mean the one who sings while walking like an ostrich. Good. I mean that Beyoncé too.

And you're telling me that there's a physically identical person called Mrs Carter? She could make a fortune doing lookalikes on the conference circuit. She could, if there was such a person. But what I'm actually telling you is that Beyoncé is calling herself Mrs Carter for a new world tour.

How eccentric. Well, there is a reason for it. Her real name is Beyoncé Knowles-Carter, you see, following her marriage to the rapper Jay-Z.

Doesn't that make her Mrs-Z or something? No. Because his real name is Shawn Carter.

This is terribly confusing. Look, it's quite simple, really. Mainstream entertainers often reinvent themselves to keep audiences interested. Beyoncé has already passed through her "Sasha Fierce" phase, which was characterised by glamour and assertiveness.

I see. And this, perhaps, is a reference to her new sense of domesticity following the birth last January of her daughter Blue.

A reference to her domesticity? On a world tour? Maybe an ironic reference.

So should we now expect her to start pureeing carrots on stage and singing about nap routines? I don't think we should. Publicity photographs for the tour show her dressed in a kind of Louis XIV bathing costume.

Not very practical daywear. No. And her Superbowl performance on Sunday was a leather extravaganza.

Yes, I saw that. Perhaps the finest piece of ostrich-walking at a sporting event in recent memory. Indeed. And she needed it after that lip-syncing fiasco at President Obama's inauguration.

It's the size of the microphone that gives it away. I know.

So Beyonce's distinctive brand of emancipated femininity is safe for now, is it? If by that you mean dancing in high heels while singing about wanting a wedding ring, then yes it is.

Do say: "Surely she is already one of the 21st-century's greatest entertainers."

Don't say: "Surely she is already one of PepsiCo Incorporated's greatest-ever salespeople."

~ MUD ~

Age: Fractionally younger than soil and water.

Appearance: Muddy

Oh, don't tell me all the poor people who got flooded are now engulfed by mud too? Amazon needs to start doing welly boots for houses. And paying tax. But that's really another issue. No, it's not about that. It's about eating mud.

I'm sorry, what? At a restaurant serving soil in Tokyo.

Ah – I'm nodding sagely – Heston Blumenthal's done all he can in Bray and Waitrose, has he? Bumped for long enough against the limits the staid British palate will tolerate, eh? Gone off to a country happy to look a raw fish in the eye and call it lunch? Very sensible. No, this is chef Toshio Tanabe, who has started serving soil to his customers.

Oh yes, they do that at Noma in Copenhagen. It's really hazelnuts, malt and beer. Not this stuff.

You mean it's actually ... you know ... soil? Yup.

So he just shovels the stuff from the garden straight on to plates and then manages to charge a fortune to gullible pseuds, is that it? Hardly. This is lab-tested-for-safety, first-class agricultural soil from the farmlands north of Tokyo, baked, boiled, triple-filtered and mixed with gelatine to produce mud, which is then used as the basis for various dishes.

Such as? Potato and soil soup.

Of course. Salad with a soil dressing. Soil risotto with a sautéed sea bass and burdock root. Soil ice cream. Soil gratin. And soil mint tea.

Sounds … appalling. His newest dish is Soil Surprise.

Don't tell me – the surprise is there's soil in it. No, wait – that there's no soil in it. No – wait – It's a ball of mashed potato mixed with soil and topped with a soil sauce.

I'm still sticking with "appalling", I think. Very wise.

Do say: "What a wonderful earthy texture. And smell. And taste. I'd happily pay upwards of £70 a head for this."

Don't say: "I'm sorry, there seems to have been a terrible mistake. You appear to be charging me a great deal of money for A DINNER MADE OF SOIL!"

13/01/2013

~ BELGIUM ~

Age: The Romans arrived around 100BC. But fossilised waffle remains suggest inhabitation since 100,000BC.

Appearance: Just above Luxembourg and covered in chocolate, beer and statues of boys weeing.

Honestly, foreigners [shakes head in bewilderment]. So why is it in the news? It can only be because someone's unearthed a new Poirot or Tintin story. Or Magritte painting.

Ah, I had – ironically – forgotten about the third famous Belgian. So, which one is it? None of them. Belgium is in the news because Gérard Depardieu, France's most famous and Frenchest actor, is joining the ranks of many super-wealthy French nationals and moving there.

Why? In response to tax hikes by France's Socialist government. President Francois Hollande –

The one who once said: "I don't like the rich"? The very same – has pledged to tax anyone earning over €1m a year at 75%. So Depardieu's outta there. He's returned his passport and social security and is going to live in a village just over the Belgian border, where the top rate is 50% for anyone earning over €34,330.

That n'est pas très cool. Ministers and many of the public certainly think that. Gallic scorn has been poured on him ever since he announced his plans to head for the Low (tax) Countries.

Ooh, I love a bit of Gallic scorn! What did his detractors say? Prime Minister Jean-Marc Ayrault called him "pathetic" and described the people who are self-exiling as "not those who are scared of becoming poor [but those] who want to get even richer", before adding: "We cannot fight poverty if those with the most, and sometimes with a lot, do not show solidarity and a bit of generosity."

I think I might love Prime Minister Ayrault a little bit. Depardieu does not feel the same. He responded in a letter published in the Journal du Dimanche, saying: "We no longer have the same homeland, I am a true European, a citizen of the world, as my father always taught me to believe."

"A citizen of wherever in the world I have to pay least to support those less fortunate than I," does he mean? Well, put it this way – I don't think any socialist subtext got lost in translation.

Do say: "But you look like a giant potato! They're going to turn you into *moules frites* over there!"

Don't say: "They should remake it as Manon des Taxed-at-Sources."

17/12/2012

~ WILBUR SMITH ~

Age: 79.

Appearance: Maths teacher on safari.

Ah, yes – I've heard of this guy. He writes novels about people having sex in Africa. Set in the past. Occasionally they escape from jackals between shags. Is that right? No.

Oh. Well, I mean it's not always jackals. Sometimes it might be pirates or hippos. Look, you've got the wrong end of the stick. What I mean is that Smith won't actually be writing them any more. At least not every word.

What? First it's Katie Price, now this! Is nothing sacred? No, it isn't. According to various reports, Smith's new publisher HarperCollins is going to pay him £15m to come up with six plot outlines, some of which will be written up by other people over the next three years.

That's very nice of HarperCollins. It certainly is. "My fans have made it very clear that they would like to read my novels and revisit my family of characters faster than I can write them," Smith says. "For them, I am willing to make a change to my working methods."

How noble. Still, it's hardly easy to devise a new bestseller, and maybe even write some of it, every six months. Not for Wilbur. As he explained to a reader in 2009: "I have never had too much trouble for creative ideas to spring up in my mind."

We'll miss his way with words. We will. Although HarperCollins has denied that the books are going to be ghost-written. According to The Bookseller, "some of the titles will be written with co-authors" but "the mechanics of the process are yet to be decided".

That doesn't sound much like denying it to me. No. And not all Smith fans are happy. One reader on his Facebook page called it "a sell out", and added: "I for one won't be buying a Wilbur book written by a third party."

Quite right! I've half a mind to start reading Wilbur Smith novels just so I can boycott them. Let's not do anything drastic. I doubt most readers will notice the difference anyway.

Really? Nah. Writing is just hackwork. Any idiot can do it.

Do say: "Hi Wilbur, could you sign my copy for me?"

Don›t say: "Thanks, but I was kind of hoping you'd do it yourself."

10/12/2012

~ VASECTOMY ~

Age: 189. The first vasectomy was carried out on a dog in 1823.

Balls! It's true. And try to treat this with the seriousness it deserves. Vasectomies on men started soon after, but didn't become widespread until the second world war.

Appearance: I'll leave that to the picture desk, who have to come up with something tasteful to illustrate this.

Why are we talking about it? Because new data shows the number of NHS vasectomies has more than halved over the past decade.

That must be down to the cuts. Look, this an extremely sensitive and important subject. The drop in the number of vasectomies is being blamed for a 10% increase in abortion rates among women over the age of 30. You take this flippant view because you are a MAN, and a pretty selfish, uncaring, wantonly sperm-spraying man at that.

Steady on. Why don't we calm down and go back to basics. What is a vasectomy? According to the NHS, it is "a minor operation during which the tubes that carry sperm from a man's testicles to the penis are cut, blocked or sealed with heat".

Bloody hell. I think I need a drink. Oh don't be so ridiculous. It's nowhere near as bad as you're making out. When you have a vasectomy, you get a local anaesthetic, go home the same day, and the bruises on your balls will disappear within a week.

Bruises on my balls!? It won't just be your balls that are bruised if you don't start seeing this from the woman's point of view. As Ann Furedi, chief executive of the British Pregnancy Advisory Service says: "Vasectomy is a safe and reliable method that gives men the opportunity to play an active role in contraception. It is disappointing that the only long-term method which enables men to play this part is declining."

OK, OK. So why are NHS vasectomies falling? Men want to keep their options open. Even once they've had five children with Belinda, they think they might want to start all over again with thirtysomething Melissa. Typical!

Man-hater! Misogynist!

Not to be confused with: Having your tonsils out.

Do say: "How much does it cost to go private?"

Don't say: "It's a snip!"

~ CHARLES DARWIN ~

Age: 73, when he died in 1882.

Appearance: Down-on-his-luck department store Santa.

Profession: English naturalist, author of *On the Origin of Species*, developer of the theory of natural selection, congressional also-ran.

Also-ran? Darwin once came second in an election for a seat in the US House of Representatives.

I never knew that. When did this happen? Last week.

But he's dead! He wasn't alone there. A dead man was elected to the Texas senate last Tuesday. Another dead guy was voted city council president of Rochester, Minnesota, and yet another won a seat on a county commission in Alabama.

OK – but he's not even an American citizen. He wasn't on the ballot either. Nevertheless, Charles Darwin received more than 4,000 write-in votes in Athens-Clark County, Georgia. The numbers from the other 24 counties in the 10th congressional district were not available at the time of writing.

Could he still win? It's unlikely. The incumbent, Republican Paul Broun, received more than 209,000 votes.

And the Democrat? Broun was running unopposed. The write-in campaign was sort of a protest.

But why Darwin? It has to do with a speech Broun gave to a church group in September in which he denounced both evolution and the big bang theory, as "lies straight from the pit of hell".

So he credits Satan with the theory of natural selection? He also said he believed the Earth is 9,000 years old, and was created in six literal days.

Perhaps his remarks were misinterpreted. There's a video of him saying it, standing in front of a wall of mounted deer heads.

I've said it before – that America is one crazy place. It gets worse – Broun is a qualified doctor, a climate-change denier and a member of the House committee on science, space and technology.

Do say: "It's shameful that in this day and age such a politician even exists."

Don't say: "Poor show, Darwin. In America, being dead is no excuse for being second best."

11/11/2012

~ NURSULTAN NAZARBAYEV ~
president of Kazakhstan

Age: 72.

Appearance: Part-time Albert Finney lookalike.

What does he do for a day job? He's the president of Kazakhstan.

As in Borat's country? That's the one.

It's an actual place? It is indeed.

I thought Sacha Baron Cohen made it up. Afraid not. He just picked a real country and caricatured it as corrupt and very silly.

So what's the real Kazakhstan like? Corrupt and very

silly. Nursultan Nazarbayevhas won two decades of widely criticised elections with around a 95% share of the vote, and even changed the law to personally exempt himself from term limits. Which may go some way to explaining why right now he is doing his best to emphasise the country's silliness.

What's he done? He has instructed Kazakh scientists to go in search of the elixir of life, and, after two years and a few million quid of research, they have invented yoghurt.

Hold on. He instructed them to what? To investigate "anti-ageing medicine, natural rejuvenation, immortality".

How did this all start? Two years ago a member of the Kazakh parliament suggested Nazarbayev stay on as president until "at least" 2020. To which he responded: "I'm willing to go on to 2020. Just find me the elixir."

As a joke, surely? Maybe at first. But he then asked Kazakh scientists to look into "the study of the prolongation of life" on three separate occasions that year, even telling them: "People of my age are really hoping all of this will happen as soon as possible."

So they brought him a yoghurt? Well, they had to bring him something. Zhaqsybai Zhumalidov, chair of the Life Sciences committee, announced their findings last week: "We have created a bio-product called Nar. It will be able to improve the quality of life and prolong it."

And Nar is a yoghurt? Yep. It's also the Kazakh word for "food". In his defence, Zhumalidov admitted there was "still work to be done".

Do say: "Look on my works, ye Mighty, and despair!"

Don't say: "Your works look a lot like Onken."

~ THE LONDON PUB ~

Age: As old as ale and man's need to quaff it in congenial company.

Appearance: Fading.

The London pub? I don't think I know that one. Is it in London? We are not talking about a single pub but a type – AKA the old-fashioned boozer.

Oh, you mean the rank and foetid oubliettes sunk along every city thoroughfare where people gather on greasy stools to drink warm pints of Old Necrosis from grubby glasses ... Um ...

... served by careworn barmaids whose memories of better days no longer even flicker in the dark depths of their melancholy eyes, all silently drowning their sorrows in a miasma of cigarette smoke and regret? No. I mean the traditional, characterful London pub, a symphony in etched glass, mahogany and brass, decades of conviviality and fond fellowship embedded in its very walls.

Actually, that's nicotine. OK, I can see we're talking about the same thing. But why? Because a group of architecture students have just submitted a 350-page document arguing that they should be given Unesco World Heritage status to protect them from demolition, renovation and takeover by the All Bar Slug and Piano.

Oh my God. Does everything in the world only exist so that it can be given UN protection under some rubric or other? Peruvian scissor dancing, Tsiattista poetic duelling and Chinese shadow puppetry have all been gathered under the shelter of the Unesco Intergovernmental Committee for the Safeguarding of Intangible Cultural Heritage. So – yes.

What does the London pub have to do join this exalted rank? It must be deemed an entity of Outstanding Universal Value by "representing a masterpiece of human creative genius".

I think the pork scratching qualifies. And contain "superlative natural phenomena".

Just supply a liver biopsy of the nearest regular. And be "bearing a unique or at least exceptional testimony to a cultural tradition".

The English have been known as drunkards since time immemorial! We're in! Let's toast our success! Mine's a pint.

Do say: "Usual please, barman."

Don't say: "A small glass of pinot grigio, please, and something chargrilled on a baguette. I'm at blond wood table 27 over there under the art."

14/10/2012

~ ROD STEWART ~

Age: 67.

Appearance: Lacquered and knackered.

Full name, including archaic, imperialist 'honour': Roderick David Stewart, CBE.

The singer? I loved his version of Solitaire. And now he's dead... That's Andy Williams! Rod's the one who gave us Da Ya Think I'm Sexy?, Tonight's the Night, You Wear it Well and Sailing. He's not dead, just shagged out.

Such a crude way of putting it. What's wrong with "tired"? It only tells half the story. As his forthcoming autobiography explains, he got tired of getting his leg over with strange women.

Strange as in two-headed? Or ... ? Women he barely knew. As he told a certain low-rent tabloid: "There was a period in my life ... where it was a bit 'one in, one out'."

I thought the expression was «in, out, in, out». But carry on. It eventually got a bit "sad", he says: "I remember being at a hotel in Cannes and we were shagging ourselves rotten, and I said, 'This is fucking depressing.'"

Just what every woman longs to hear at the moment of ecstasy. He should have tried settling down. He did, repeatedly. He has been married three times, to model Alana Hamilton, model Rachel Hunter and model Penny Lancaster, and his long-term girlfriends have included model Dee Harrington and model Kelly Emberg. He has eight children in all, two by Penny, whom he married five years ago. He was "definitely" in love with everyone he impregnated.

He still sounds just a little sleazy. Doesn't he? But although he admits he two-timed almost all his exes, they all still talk to him, except for actor Britt Ekland, who "bloody hates" him.

Actor? You mean Rod swings both ways? Britt's a woman, you idiot.

But–. The Guardian hates the word "actress". It's official policy.

Hmm. Does he have a type? Apart from models, of course. Leggy blondes.

How original. Any other pastimes? He's a keen footballer and follows Scotland, Celtic and Manchester United. He also has a giant train set in his LA mansion. Or should we talk about his music?

Of course not. It's bloody awful.

Do say: "Maggie May …"

Don't say: "… but I've never understood why any woman would."

07/10/2012

~ JAMES BOND ~

Age: 59.

Appearance: Daniel Craig, for now.

What's Bond doing these days? It's his 50th birthday.

I thought you said he was 59? Well, technically he is, if you measure from the release of the first book. But it's the 50th anniversary of the release of Dr No, the first Bond film, this Friday.

I see. So how is he going to celebrate? In typical Bond style, of course.

Quiet restaurant meal with close friends? You don't know much about James Bond, do you?

Almost nothing. Is he more of a barbecue kind of guy? No, he's more of a champagne, sports cars and lingerie models on a speedboat kind of guy.

Sports cars on a speedboat? Yup. That's just how he rolls. He also parachuted out of a helicopter with the Queen at the London Olympics opening ceremony a couple of months ago. Typical Bond style, in a nutshell, encompasses anything absurdly lavish or just lavishly absurd.

And which is he going with for his 50th? In this case he's leaning very much towards the absurd.

Oh dear. What's he doing? He has teamed up with Visit Britain to front an ad campaign luring tourists to the UK under the questionable tag-line "Bond is Great Britain". The campaign doubles up as advertising for the new Bond film Skyfall, out later this month, and will be unveiled on Friday at the same time as the film's theme song, which singer-song-writer Adele has just confirmed she has written and performed.

Doesn't sound that absurd so far. Oh, wait for it: the campaign also features an international competition offering lucky winners the chance to visit Britain and "Live Like Bond".

Ah. What would living like Bond be, exactly? Well, judging by the films, frequent life-threatening violence, sex with near-strangers in expensive hotels and plenty of trips to exotic locations a lot more exciting than the rainy old UK.

Not the best slogan ever then. No, but it is a step up from the previous "Live Like Voldemort" campaign.

They really did that? No, obviously not.

Do say: "You only visit Britain twice."

Don't say: "The UK is not enough."

02/10/2012

HOT BATHS

Age: Ancient.

Appearance: Bubbly.

That's nice. I love a long, hot bath with a book and a cup of tea. Who doesn't?

Cats. But otherwise, sure. It's like being back in the womb, but with a book and a cup of tea. And it's good for you. Better than exercise!

Really? Well, in one narrow way, based on a single study with a small sample, perhaps.

I see. How do we know this? Some scientist called Dr Steve Faulkner did this experiment at Loughborough University where he fitted 10 unfit males with rectal thermometers and other devices, then got them to have long, hot, relaxing baths.

I think I'd be more relaxed without the thermometer. You get used to it. After the bath, the men got a meal, and on another day they did some vigorous cycling instead of the bath.

And? Much to everyone's surprise, the bathers had peak blood sugar levels after eating that were 10% lower than the cyclists'. In short, the study suggests that hot baths might do a better job than exercise at lowering your blood sugar, which is the challenge in diabetes. The theory is that it is something to do with "heat shock proteins".

Fantastic! When I develop diabetes, I'll remember that. Controlling peak blood sugar may also prevent diabetes. Plus, having a long, hot bath was found to increase calorie burning by 80%. Nowhere near as much as cycling, but still useful. In an hour in a hot bath, the men each burned 126 calories, which is about the same as a half-hour walk.

So, quick recap: science says I can stop doing exercise and eat whatever I like as long as I have plenty of baths? No. Science says: "We would always encourage increased physical activity and exercise as the best way to maintain good health." Faulkner does, anyway.

How about the risks, such as slipping over on the tiles or getting wrinkly toes? Don't baths also poach your testicles and stop you having children? Some research suggests they may.

What if you've already got, arguably, too many children? Then I suppose the bath is the perfect place to hide.

Do say: "I like to arrange scented candles around the room to create my own peaceful sanctum. Bliss."

Don't say: "Until someone needs the toilet."

21/08/2016

~ TRANSCRANIAL DIRECT CURRENT STIMULATION (TDCS) ~

Age: Available, in one form or another, for well over 100 years.

Appearance: Homemade, last-minute Frankenstein's monster Halloween costume.

What is it? It's the application of direct electrical current to the brain.

You mean like tasering someone? No – it's a constant current, delivered through electrodes attached to the scalp.

More like the electric chair, then. Except the current used is very weak; devices are usually powered by a nine-volt battery.

So it's for minor crimes? It's not a punishment, it's a treatment.

Seriously? For what? It's meant to improve cognitive ability, enhance memory and increase attention span.

I see. And how does that work? It doesn't, apparently.

You're saying that plugging someone's brain into a portable phone charger doesn't actually make them smarter? You surprise me. It's worse than that – a new study published in the journal Behavioural Brain Research suggests that tDCS has a statistically detrimental effect on IQ.

It makes you dumber? It's just one study, but in research, findings about the benefits of tDCS have been, shall we say, mixed.

Who ever thought this was a good idea? A form of electrical brain stimulation was first used to treat melancholy in the 19th century.

Melancholy isn't even a thing. In the 1960s, tDCS became briefly fashionable when it was shown that it could alter the excitability of neurons in the motor cortex. More recently, it's been used to increase or decrease cortical activity with the aim of alleviating depression or insomnia.

Hopefully, doctors will exercise extreme caution with the treatment now the possibility of detrimental effects has been raised. Are you kidding? People are out there zapping themselves – you can buy a tDCS kit online for less than £100. You can even find instructions to make your own.

So this isn't the end for tDCS? Probably not. And a similar application, but with alternating current – tACS – is also being researched.

Do say: "The effect of electrical stimulation on the brain has fascinated scientists for centuries, and yet it remains so little understood."

Don't say: "My IQ's gone down? I'm shocked."

05/05/2015

~ @BRITISHMONARCHY ~

Appearance: Stuffy-chic.

Age: Seven years.

I'm no historian, but I'm pretty sure I remember there being a British monarchy more than seven years ago. Oh, it's more than 1,000 years old, dear boy. What we're talking about, however, is @BritishMonarchy, the Queen's Twitter account, which was started in April 2009.

Ah. I thought she was @Queen_UK? No, that's what's known as a parody account. Some comedian pretends to be the Queen in order to crack jokes and sell T-shirts.

I see. Actually, that explains quite a lot. Is @BritishMonarchy obsessed with gin as well? Not really. It's more obsessed with the royal family visiting dull things.

Ah yes. I've just checked. At the moment, it seems to be obsessed with bandstands and commemorative plaques. Yeah, that's about right. Although it could all change soon.

How come? The palace is advertising for a new head of digital engagement.

What's that? It's someone to run its website, YouTube channel, Facebook page and Twitter account. The job pays an annual salary of £45,000–£50,000.

I'm their man! I'm great at the Facebook. Really? Can you find "new ways to maintain the Queen's presence in the public eye and on the world stage"?

Instagramming corgis? Spat with Kanye? Sex tape? Um … Are you at least "a natural communicator, influential and with a genuine user focus"?

Oh, definitely. People are always saying how genuine my user focus is. "You'll liaise with a broad spectrum of stakeholders on a daily basis and will drive change through collaboration." Are you sure you can handle that?

Where's the joy in liaising with stakeholders if you can't do it every day? I suppose.

One thing: I have a gender and an ethnicity, which I'm worried may go against me at the interview stage. That won't be a problem. The monarchy are "proud to champion diversity throughout the organisation". They say: "Our approach to recruitment and selection is fair, open and based purely on merit."

A hereditary monarchy that is committed to recruitment purely on merit? Is there a problem with that?

Not that I can see. Excellent.

20/04/2016

~ HD164595 b ~

Age: 4.5 billion years, give or take.

Appearance: Not visible to the naked eye.

Sounds like you don't know too much about it. That's because it hasn't been up to much until now.

What exactly are we talking about? A sun-sized star 94.4 light years from Earth, in the constellation of Hercules.

How interesting can it be if no one has bothered to give it a proper name? Well, it has an apparent magnitude of 7.075, a similar mass and temperature to our own sun, and a Neptune-sized planet, HD164595 b, in its orbit.

Whoop de doo. And someone from out that way may be trying to get in touch.

What are you talking about? In May 2015, a strong radio signal coming from the vicinity of HD164595 was detected at the Ratan-600 observatory in Russia.

Why are we only hearing about it now? Because it is due to be made public in a forthcoming presentation, leading to speculation that the signal could be coming from a transmitter built by a Type I civilisation.

You mean ET phoned from home? Maybe.

Really? No.

Stop toying with me! While it is conceivable the signal was sent by aliens, scientists from the Search for Extraterrestrial Intelligence (Seti) remain sceptical.

That's their job, I suppose. No one has been able to replicate the findings so far, even though many of the world's telescopes have been trained on the vicinity in the last few days.

Absence of evidence isn't evidence of absence. No, but a one-off signal is more consistent with something such as a stellar flare, or radio interference here on Earth.

You just have to believe, otherwise ET won't call back. And even if aliens were pointing the signal directly at us, the transmitting power required would equal the total energy consumption of all humankind.

So it's possible. But there is no reason to think they even know we're here.

They can see our TV! They'll be wanting Seinfeld explained to them! HD164595 is 94 light years away. None of our TV has reached there yet.

Thanks for ruining this for me. Any time.

Do say: "HELLO FROM PLANET EARTH. NO NEED TO REPLY IF YOU'RE SLIMY."

Don't say: "SPOILER ALERT: CHANDLER AND MONICA EVENTUALLY GET IT TOGETHER."

31/08/2016

~ JEREMY PAXMAN ~

Age: 66.

Appearance: Easter Island statue meets missing Mount Rushmore head.

I knew it! Emily Maitlis just isn't cutting it, is she? He's coming back to Newsnight, riding in on a white stallion of hard news and pointless adversariality, if that is indeed a word! No, he's not.

Oh. He's in a spat with a free newspaper aimed at the over-50s called the *Mature Times*.

Oh crikey. What has he said now? He took issue with an issue he found in a hotel lobby and wrote that "mature" meant "on the verge of incontinence, idiocy and peevish valetudinarianism".

I've missed him. And he called it a "dreary publication" full of adverts for "hearing aids, reclining chairs, copper insoles, stairlifts, devices to help you in and out of the bath [and] cruises somewhere in the company of other virtual corpses", as if this is all older people are interested in.

Are they not? Well, he's not. You wouldn't be either, if you conceived of other people your own age as virtual corpses on the verge of incontinence, idiocy and peevish valetudinarianism.

I wouldn't want them leaving great patches of peevish valetudinarianism on the sofa, that's for sure. Has the publisher of *Mature Times* taken this lying down? Perhaps on one of his recliner chairs? He has not. Andrew Silk has come out fighting against the man who suggested the publication be renamed "The Surgical Stocking Sentinel" or "Winceyette Weekly".

Do tell. He likened Paxman to Jeremy Clarkson without the charisma or money.

Ooh! Sick burn, as I believe the young folk say! It's pretty good, isn't it? He's also called on him to apologise to the 21m over-50s in the country.

Oh, can't they take a joke? Paxo also called them "humour-less".

Ah. And he said there was a good argument for banning them from EU referendums and the like: "It's simply not fair to allow people to vote for a future they won't live to enjoy or endure."

I miss him more and more. Maybe he will come back to Newsnight yet. Semi-retirement does seem to be leaving him with idle hands.

Do say: "I would totally buy Winceyette Weekly."

Don't say: "Eh? What? Speak UP, young man!"

30/08/2016

Pass Notes